If my house were on fire...

...these are the recipes I'd take!

by Lori Powell Gordon

Adventure Publications, Inc.
Cambridge, MN

This book is dedicated to the person who thought to tape an upside-down plastic spoon to the pen so people wouldn't walk off with it. They deserve more.

And also to my Mom, who taught me not to be afraid of the kitchen.

I'd like to thank all the Little People: Dick, who helped me proofread; John and Mike, for help with the computer; Peter, who got me started; Cory, for bringing a scanner to my house and hooking it up; Bonita and Stan, for talking me through this; my junior high English teacher, Mrs. Nelson; all the people who don't sue me because I borrowed their recipes—if they have something to sell, please buy it; anybody who buys this book and doesn't give it to the Goodwill; my dogs, Brandy and the late Rosie, for letting me roll the computer chair over their tails and not biting me and for not dribbling too much in their sleep.

Thanks, also, to everybody at Adventure Publications. They're all good sports.

Design by Jonathan Norberg

Copyright 2002 by Lori Powell Gordon
Adventure Publications, Inc.
820 Cleveland Street South
Cambridge, MN 55008
1-800-678-7006
ISBN 1-59193-003-0

Table of Contents

Beverages

Cindy's Iced Tea

2 tea bags or 2 tablespoons instant tea
2 cups boiling water
¾ cup sugar
¼ cup lemon juice
2 cups cold water
½ teaspoon almond or vanilla extract

Mix tea and boiling water and let stand for 5 minutes. Remove tea bags. Add sugar and lemon juice. Add cold water and almond or vanilla extract. Serve over ice.

I have to admit it, I still like that Lipton iced tea with lemon and sugar. There are certain times when it is just perfect, and if you make real iced tea and add lemon and sugar to it, you will embarrass yourself with how many of those little sugar packages you have to add. This recipe is from my friend Cindy Writesman in Missouri. It's really old, but I like it, and it is just a little more sophisticated than the Lipton stuff, so your friends won't think you have the tastebuds of a dumpster. Go ahead and make it with honey if you like. I'm just giving it to you as it was given to me.

Sweet Herbal Iced Tea

4 herbal tea bags (mint blend, rosehip blend,
   whatever you like)
6 cups boiling water
12 oz. can of frozen lemonade, cherry, apple or
   white grape juice

**Put tea bags in a tea pot and pour water over them. Let brew
until water is lukewarm. Remove tea bags, pour tea into a large
pitcher and add undiluted frozen juice concentrate. Stir and
chill. Serve over ice.**

**Note: I don't mean to be vague, but you can hardly screw up on
the combinations here. I like a tea that has mint and licorice
with lemonade concentrate. One of those red, lemony hibiscus
blend teas is good with cherry or white grape juice. A spice tea
is nice with apple juice. Use your imagination. If you save a few
of the original bottles the tea comes in at the grocery store,
wash and refill them, your kids will never know....**

My kids like to buy those expensive
bottles of iced tea with all the herbs
and healthy ingredients that improve
your energy and memory. You'd think
they'd remember that they just spent
a half hour's wage on something they
could make at home for almost nothing, but the herbs aren't *that* good.

Lisa's Margaritas

⅔ cup each tequila and lime juice
⅓ cup each Triple Sec and water
¼ cup superfine sugar
ice*
lime slices
coarse salt

In a blender container that holds at least 5 cups of liquid, place tequila, lime juice, Triple Sec, water and sugar. Add enough ice to bring liquid level to 5 cups. Blend at highest speed until ice is finely crushed. Rub edges of 6 chilled goblets or wine glasses with lime wedges. Dip rims in coarse salt. Fill glasses with margaritas. Garnish with lime slices. 6 servings.

*It's best to use crushed ice unless you have a very good blender. Crushing ice cubes can wreck the average blender and dull the blades.

The secret to entertaining is to make it look like you were expecting company.

I am stealing this recipe from my friend Lisa Schroeder's cookbook, *Sizzling Southwestern Cookery*, because I don't think she'll mind, and if she does, she'll call me, and I probably won't be so embarrassed and ashamed that I feel like eating an entire carton of coffee ice cream with homemade hot fudge sauce and (salted) pecans, for more than a couple of days. These are perfect for summer evenings so hot you want to sit around in a cotton dress with no underwear. Unless you're a guy, in which case you should sit around in your underwear and no cotton dress. It's also OK to invite your friends over to sit in their underwear. Just make sure you complain not only about the heat, but also the humidity.

Spicy Rosemary Lemonade

1 cup water
1 cup sugar
2 teaspoons fresh rosemary leaves, or 1 teaspoon dried
½ teaspoon dried red chili, crushed
3 cups water
⅔ cup lemon juice
thin lemon slices

In a small saucepan, bring water, sugar, rosemary and crushed chili to a boil; boil 5 minutes. Strain mixture and cool. In a large pitcher, pour the 3 cups water and lemon juice. Add cooled syrup and stir well. Serve over ice and garnish with lemon slices.

I like this recipe because it surprised our friend John Stoklosa. He and my husband have a history of being overly macho when it comes to red peppers, but even John was unsure if it was ethical to put them in lemonade. I stole this recipe from Lisa, so I'm still sorry.

Chai

5⅓ cups water
2⅔ cups milk
8 teaspoons sugar
6 slices fresh ginger
3" piece of stick cinnamon
8 whole cardamom pods, split
6 teaspoons Darjeeling tea

Bring everything except tea to a boil. Add tea, cover and steep. Strain and serve, hot or iced.

You may still be ordering your double skinny latte with legs, but there are those predicting that tea will be the next big beverage trend. Whatever. If you enjoy a Chai tea or two at the shops, try making it at home. It's actually a very old traditional East Indian recipe.

Bulb Dreams

In the silence of winter when the
world lies under thick quilts of
snow,
In the dead sleep of winter when
nature waits,
In the long moaning winter when
branches outside my window
Creak stiffly or not at all,
The sap pulled deep inside,
Looking for warmth beneath the
snow.
In the hush of winter when I
forget all colors but black and white,
I thirst for blue and green,
I hunger after lavender and
fuchsia.
In the crystal cold of winter, I nest
in flannel and down,
And close my eyes to the early
darkness,
Feel only the glow of the
woodstove on my cheek,
I test the night air with my toe
And pull it back.

In the still secret of winter
I dream of gardens planted and
forgotten.
I dream of the old lady Mary who
was my neighbor,
And grew flowers wild and tame
until the cold got in her bones.
In my dream she lives in California
With a yard full of roses,
hollyhocks and tulips,
Delphiniums and asters,
Daylilies and Dutchman's
breeches.
Mary is showing me around and
smiling.
But I know I should get home,
Unless I miss the blooming
Of my own garden.

Tom and Jerrys

1 dozen eggs—room temperature
pinch of salt
2 lb. pkg. powdered sugar
1 teaspoon vanilla
some kind of intoxicant
whole nutmeg, for grating

Beat egg whites until stiff. Add salt. Add 1 lb. sugar and beat some more. Beat egg yolks until thick, add vanilla, 1 lb. sugar and beat until mixture is light yellow. Fold both together. Store in refrigerator. To serve, put some batter in a cup with a shot of rum, brandy or whatever you like, we are not purists here. Fill cup with boiling water. Sprinkle with freshly grated nutmeg. I think the fresh nutmeg is pretty important. If you find yourself grating your fingertips, maybe you should lay off the Tom and Jerrys.

Stay as far away as possible from grouchy people.

I'm thinking about Christmas, so of course, I have to put this in. You can now buy those eggs that are raw, but have been nuked; so you decide if raw eggs or radiation is your greater risk. I refuse to be your mother.

My Frozen Cappuccinos

1½ heaping teaspoons instant coffee powder,
   regular or decaf
2 heaping teaspoons raw or regular sugar, or to taste
4 heaping teaspoons powdered milk
½ cup water
6 ice cubes, crushed

Put it all in the blender and give it a buzz.

Note: These are heaping teaspoons, not really measuring spoons. Makes one serving.

If your dog has one flea it
probably has one thousand.

One summer I became addicted, not to Tom and Jerrys, because really, it was summer—get a grip—but to those icy blended coffee drinks sold at the big coffee chains. They would help me sail down Interstate 35 to Des Moines, singing wildly with Bonnie Raitt on the radio. This is not their recipe, but it is pretty close and has that same kind of icy grittiness that I find so intriguing in their version.

Lyle

I am a fan of Lyle Lovett—the country western, blues, jazz genius with big hair and a crooked smile. I'm also the happily married mother of two, with a lovely house, a cabin, two dogs, two cats, a horse, several fish and an African pygmy hedgehog. I'm a good cook, have a successful career and an assortment of interesting, mentally balanced friends.

And I am powerless over Lyle.

I had a neighbor, Gloria Moe, who was this way about the Beatles when we were 10. When George Harrison would sing: "If this is love, you've got to give me more," it sounded like mo—because he's English—and Gloria would go weak. I thought it was so dumb.

In college, I had a job in a fabric store where mostly I sat and read *Redbook* magazine's condensed versions of romance novels while I waited for someone to come in to buy a pattern for a jumpsuit. There was a woman who came in every day. She had some kind of degenerative disease that made it difficult to walk, but I think her mind was OK. Except that perhaps the loneliness and desperation of her condition had turned her into the most avid fan you could imagine of The Captain and Tenille. I was trapped in my cubicle of counter and cash register, pinned to my stool by her endless ramblings about the crooners of "Muskrat Love." (Or was that the Carpenters? Whatever.)

I'm not that way about Lyle. Only my closest friends know that he is on my fantasy birthday party list. The other guests are Julia Child, because she's legendary; Mr. Rogers, because he's accepting; and Dr. Ruth, because she's...short. It would be quite a party. Julia would cook and Dr. Ruth would dangle her feet off the edge of the chair and I would talk and Lyle would listen and Mr. Rogers would smile and tell us we were special.

I know what people said about Lyle. So he has big hair. So his mouth goes up on one side and down on the other. So he's kind of skinny and he always wears suits on stage and he never knows what to do with his hands when he's not playing the guitar.

I know people said, what did She see in him. I'd say, what did He see in her, but I respect Lyle too much to do that. I'm sure she's a wonderful person. On this point I have to trust Lyle. (I won't even bring it up at my party.)

I bought tickets to his concert. My husband went with me. He's such a sport; it must be difficult to sit next to someone who brings one of those suitcases with the wheels and the handle that pulls out, not a real big one, just to hold enough clothes for two or three days in case Lyle asks if there are any 42-year-old women who would like to join him on the tour. I would be up that aisle so fast those wheels would smoke, and I am sure Lyle would like me. He would have to like me. And I, being a mature adult, would not just admire him as a star but come to know and like him as a person, happily ever after, the end.

Wait.

Back to the tickets. I know Lyle will always send me complimentary tickets when our friendship blooms, but this time I purchased two. One for me and one for Dick. Someone would have to drive the car home.

When the night of the concert came, we arrived at the theater early. Mostly we wanted a place to park in a ramp; it was cold out and even the most avid fan must be practical. Could Lyle respect me if I waited outside his hotel in the frigid air? Don't be silly.

Our early arrival provided me with the opportunity to determine just who else attends Lyle Lovett concerts; and granted, we were in the more expensive seats, and I'm sure there were a lot of pierced club types in the balcony that I couldn't see. Down below, it was pretty much middle-aged women with men who were beginning to bald. Sure, there were a few really beautiful younger women, but I know they were mindless. Some of them weren't even wearing turtlenecks.

And then Lyle came on stage. I listened to him and the large band, and I wondered, why is this the sexiest man alive?

Because he and his whole band wear suits? Because he listens to his excellent musicians? Because he doesn't wear his hat inside? Because his music and lyrics are brilliant? Because he doesn't know where to put his hands and he reminds you of every goofy guy you failed to notice until he became a neurosurgeon or a rodeo cowboy or invented the personal computer?

Yeah, I thought, as I wheeled my suitcase back to the car, where I happily rode home with Dick. Lyle's all of that, and I'm the best friend Lyle doesn't know he has.

BEVERAGES 17

Mexican Hot Chocolate

1 cup sugar
2 tablespoons plus 1 teaspoon cornstarch
½ cup water
4 cups milk
2 squares unsweetened chocolate
½ teaspoon almond extract
½ teaspoon ground cinnamon

Mix sugar, cornstarch and water in a medium saucepan and stir until smooth. Whisk in the milk and chocolate and simmer for 10 minutes until it is thick and smooth. It will be almost as thick as pudding. Stir in extract and cinnamon. Serve hot. Don't burn your mouth.

If you need four-wheel drive, you should probably stay home and make doughnuts.

This hot chocolate always reminds me of the time Dick left for work in a snowstorm. It was about an hour later when he came back into the house and said he hadn't gotten to the end of the driveway yet. I think I would have come in sooner. Anyway, I was making Mexican hot chocolate and doughnut holes. This is an excellent combination. A more authentic combination is hot chocolate and churros, but they take a little more work and you have to roll your Rs. I'll give you that recipe in my advanced cookbook.

Appetizers

A Note About Appetizers

Appetizers don't do anything for your appetite except eliminate it, so I don't really approve of them before dinner. Why would you want to cook a wonderful meal and have your guests sit down bloated with chips and salsa? One reason is because you forgot to cook the dinner due to the fact that you were lounging around in the tub all day eating bonbons and reading *People* magazine's most recent article about Chuck and Camilla. This is perfectly understandable; it could happen to anyone, and your guests will be so fascinated with your prune-like fingertips they will forget that it is ten o'clock and they're still eating cheese and crackers.

The only gastronomically appropriate time to serve appetizers, in my humble opinion, is when you are planning no meal except appetizers (and probably dessert, because you didn't really eat anything, right?). So, I'll give you one recipe—well, maybe two—you don't think I plan these things, do you?

Italian Roasted Sweet Peppers

olive oil
red, yellow and green sweet peppers
sweet yellow onions
black pepper
capers
anchovies, minced or paste

Heat olive oil over medium heat in an ovenproof pan. Add peppers, which have been seeded and cut lengthwise into slivers, and sliced onions. Cook over high heat until they become limp. Discard excess liquid, season with pepper and add some capers and anchovies. Cook over medium heat until anchovies are completely dissolved. Place the pan in 400° oven and let pepper mixture cook, uncovered, until the peppers look and smell roasted and have dried out a bit. Be sure to turn them over 2 or 3 times so they don't burn. Serve warm or at room temperature with crusty French bread.

It is just possible that your mother was right.

I think you know how I feel about appetizers by now. Think of this as part of a meal, as an antipasto if you will; don't think of it in the same category as shrimp dip.

🔥 How to **Teach** a **Man** to **Dance**

Don't laugh. This is a serious problem. It goes like this: You meet a guy, and you're both eager to make a good impression. There is music playing; he asks you to dance. You go to the dance floor, gyrate around a little, and it's fine. Then he asks you out again. You discover you enjoy each other's company and spend more and more time together, but you never go dancing again. You see, he really doesn't like to dance, but the relationship progresses anyway and you get married. He still doesn't like to dance, but now it's different. It becomes creepy. You want him to be able to dance, but you realize he can't even tap his toe to music. You try dancing together, but you find yourself leading because you can't stand dancing with someone who can't dance, and you want him to be a guy who *can* dance.

You have two choices. You can never dance again in your life. You'll go home early from all the weddings and parties, or sit back and watch the young people dancing. Or, you can dance with your male gay friends, who all dance beautifully. (Okay, I don't want to be discriminatory toward the gay guys who like to hunt and play football, but I feel you really are in the minority.) Dancing with your gay friends has another benefit—you can always go shopping just before or after the dancing—but it's not the same. A gay guy is not really who you want to be dancing with, and don't let it break your heart, dear, but *you're* not exactly who he was hoping for either. So what do you do?

Teach your spouse to dance! It's fun! It's easy! It can be done! Just follow these simple steps.

1. Find some music he really likes. He should help you out on this one. It can be that guy who sang "The Green Beret" *(fighting soldiers from the sky...dadadada who fight and die...ten thousand men will fight today, but only one wins the green beret...)*. Or it could be the Davy Crockett theme song from when he was a kid. It doesn't matter. Sit him down on the couch and put the song on the CD player. (Maybe it has to be a record player if it's Davy Crockett.) Turn it up. Tell him not to move until he gets a beat, then kind of rock back and forth to the music. His feet probably shouldn't even

be involved at this point. Try some other music he likes. Watch him until he is rocking in a fashion that seems to have something to do with the beat. Enough for today. Give him a beer and do something else he thinks is fun.

2. Put on some music he likes and you think has an identifiable beat. Ask him to stand next to you. Explain this simple fact. All dancing is like walking. You move your feet left right left right left right. You never go right right left right left left, or anything like that. It's *always* left right left right. This may seem simple to you, but it will be news to a lot of guys. Give him time to absorb this information. Ask him to shift his weight from one foot to the other in time to the music. Left right left right. Now begin walking around the room. Remind him to move his feet in the left right sequence. When this is going well, try sometimes taking a longer step and sometimes taking a shorter step. Take a couple of long steps. Take a couple of short steps. Point out to him that he may have to pause for just a fraction of a second when he takes the tiny steps so the music has a chance to catch up. Try to stay in time with the music. Good. Have a beer.

3. Find an old recording of the song "Color My World." Remember this one? The classic slow dance song? If you can't find it, find something else that is slow and romantic. Ask your spouse to close his eyes and rock back and forth to the music. When he seems to be doing this successfully, stand in front of him and put your arms around his neck and have him put his arms on your waist. This assumes he is a little bit taller than you. Otherwise, you work it out. Do the rocking back and forth from one foot to the other kind of dance. Now try the ballroom dance hand position: Put your left hand on his right shoulder. Have him put his right hand behind your waist. Tell him that this will be how he will steer you like a car—these kind of mental images will help. With your elbows bent, hold his left hand with your right hand. Stand like this until he stops sweating. Now have a beer or whatever.

4. Resume the ballroom dance position and try rocking back and forth to "Color My World" in this position. Now get out of bed and try this standing up.

5. Put on some old Frank Sinatra music. The one where he sings with Nancy is nice too, and it's kind of funny to boot. It's good to keep your sense of humor nourished during these exercises so you don't become violent. Discover together how you can say the words, "Long, long, short, short," quietly in your partner's ear.

6. From here you're on your own. Keep whispering. Keep moving those feet. Have a beer.

Cheese Wafers

½ lb. grated Swiss or a mixture of cheeses
  (doesn't Swiss cheese make your tongue itch?)
½ lb. soft butter
1 cup flour, sifted, more if needed
¼ teaspoon pepper
pinch of cayenne
salt to taste—this will depend on the type of cheese you use
1 egg
some extra grated cheese for topping

Preheat oven to 425°.

Knead first six ingredients together in a bowl. Roll 1 tablespoon in a ball and flatten into a cake ¼" thick. Bake 10–15 minutes on a buttered baking sheet to see how it holds together.* It should spread slightly, puff lightly and brown. If it spreads more than you like, or is too fragile, add a little more flour. When satisfied, form rest of dough and place on baking sheet. Paint tops with 1 egg beaten with ½ teaspoon of water and top each with a pinch of grated cheese. Bake 10–15 minutes until puffed and browned. Cool on a rack.

*I know it will take an extra 10 minutes out of your busy life to get the flour right. The deal is, some cheeses are fattier than others, and you are going to try different cheeses, right? So quit whining. You will like this.

This is a recipe from Sande McGee Lavin McGee, my sister-in-law's sister. I don't think that really is her last name, but it kind of matches both her marital history and her relationship to me. Make them to serve with cold beer, a nice white wine, or the ever-charming margarita.

Never consider marriage until you have successfully kept a houseplant.

Salads

🔥 Tips for Healthy Eating

1. Eat when you are hungry. Don't eat because you might get hungry sometime later in the day and you don't want to be hungry because it's been so long since you've *been* hungry that you've forgotten if it's really bad or not. Wait. You can handle it.

2. Stop eating before you have to dial 911.

3. If you are really hungry for something, eat it. Don't eat everything else that's kind of like it, but not quite, so you still want some. Just don't eat six quarts of it. Remember, you will have another chance to eat again, later. We all only have one last meal in our lives.

4. On the other hand, if there is something that you cannot keep your mouth off of, you'd better not have it in the house. It's OK to go out to a restaurant to eat these things, because there you will experience a kind of social humiliation portion control. It's hard to imagine yourself saying to a waitress, "Gee, that chocolate pecan cheesecake was so good, I think I'll have a second piece." No. We only do that in the glow of our own refrigerator light.

One time I went on the AT&T diet. That meant I could eat whatever I wanted whenever the phone rates were cheap—after 11:00 p.m. on weekdays and from 11:00 p.m. Fridays until 5:00 p.m. Sundays. It's a diet that might work for you.

Chinese Chicken Salad

¼ cup soy sauce
2 tablespoons honey
1 clove garlic
3 boneless, skinless chicken breast halves
4 cups water, boiling
2 tablespoons oil
2 green onions, chopped
1 slice fresh ginger, chopped
½ teaspoon red pepper flakes
½ teaspoon chili paste with garlic
1 teaspoon peppercorn salt*
6 cups salad greens of your choice
garnishes: shredded carrot, chopped peanuts,
   diced red bell pepper

When I finished college with a degree in art, my dad told me if I didn't get a job, he'd find me one. The job he found was as a secretary. Kay Clint, who ran the United Way in town, had her desk next to mine. She gave me this recipe for Chinese Chicken Salad.

Combine soy sauce, honey and garlic and set aside. Put chicken in boiling water and cook over medium heat 15 minutes. Remove from heat and let stand 20 minutes. Cool and shred. Heat oil and add onions, ginger, red pepper flakes, chili paste and peppercorn salt. Fry 1 minute and add to soy sauce mixture. Put chicken on salad greens, toss with dressing, garnish as desired.

*Brown 2 tablespoons peppercorns with ¼ cup salt. Crush and store in a covered jar.

Watercress and Orange Salad

Dressing:
3 tablespoons canola oil
2 tablespoons fresh orange juice, or frozen orange juice
    concentrate for more intense flavor
1 tablespoon sesame oil
2 teaspoons sugar
1 teaspoon grated orange peel (use an organic orange)
½ teaspoon salt
¼ teaspoon black pepper

Salad:
2 bunches watercress
1 orange
¼ pound (about 1 cup) jicama,* peeled and cut into match-
    stick pieces
1 tablespoon chopped crystallized ginger
2 teaspoons toasted sesame seeds

**Blend dressing in blender. Set aside. Break watercress into 2"
pieces, discarding any tough stems. Peel orange. Cut crosswise
into ¼" slices and cut each slice into quarters. Place watercress, orange and jicama in salad bowl. Pour dressing over
salad and toss. Sprinkle with ginger and sesame seeds.**

***Jicama is brown paper bag colored and is kind of like a cross
between a water chestnut and a green apple. It's often about the
size and shape of a grapefruit. If you're afraid of unusual produce, try a peeled granny smith apple, but think about nuclear
waste—*now there is something you should be afraid of.***

I found this recipe in my file. I can't
remember who gave it to me, but the
handwriting looks suspiciously like
Pegi Lee (not the singer, the mom), or
Cindy. One of my secret testers tried it
and they said it was wonderful—
watercress, oranges, jicama, ginger.

Labor of Love Salad

romaine lettuce and watercress
crumbled gorgonzola cheese (an Italian blue cheese)
walnuts (it would be nice if you toasted them)
fresh basil
equal parts of olive oil and balsamic vinegar

Wash and dry the lettuce and watercress. Tear them up and toss them with the rest of the ingredients.

Whistling girls are like crowing hens.
(Grandma Underhill)

I'm not sure I've actually made this salad yet, but I'm sure when I do it will be terrific. I surreptitiously tore it out of a magazine in the dentist's office. It is supposedly from some famous restaurant and will induce labor in overdue women.

Three Tomato Salad

red cherry tomatoes, quartered
yellow pear tomatoes, quartered
ripe, slightly yellow tomatillos, quartered
slivers of fresh basil
extra virgin olive oil
balsamic vinegar
freshly ground black pepper

The key here is that the tomatoes are just out of the garden, the basil is fresh, and you sprinkle on the olive oil and vinegar and grind on some fresh pepper. You could put baby greens under it all, if you like.

Once, Dick and I were on a food pilgrimage in California and we ate at Chez Panisse, sort of a Bethlehem for foodies. They served a simple, lovely salad that tasted like this.

Tomato and Tarragon Salad

ripe, fresh summer tomatoes, sliced or chunked
homemade croutons, preferably made from whole wheat
   bread, cut into 1" squares, slowly sautéed in olive oil and
   garlic, sprinkled with seasoned salt
mayonnaise
fresh tarragon

**Cut up the tomatoes. Make about ⅓ as many croutons as you
have tomatoes. Mix these together with mayonnaise and
chopped fresh tarragon. The dressing should coat the tomatoes
in a rather plentiful fashion. Season with salt and pepper to
taste. You will think you are in heaven.**

Cindy, who calls often with odd
requests like, "I have a deer's heart
and two gallon buckets of fresh morel
mushrooms. What should I do with
them?" is really an excellent cook.
This is her concept. It's never really
been written down as an official
recipe. It is wonderful just the way it
is or on a bed of bitter salad greens.

Baby Greens with Warm Shiitake Dressing

fresh shiitake mushrooms
sea salt or coarse salt*
balsamic vinegar
olive oil
freshly ground black pepper
pecan pieces, toasted
baby salad greens
chevre (goat cheese)

My friends Greg and Peter told me about eating this at a restaurant. I have no idea if my recipe tastes the same as what they had, but it is delicious. (Don't be skimpy with the shiitakes, OK?)

Slice the shiitakes into strips and sauté them in a little olive oil. Sprinkle them with coarse salt. Put some baby greens on a plate and decorate them with little blobs of chevre. (I just poke a big hole in the plastic tube it comes in and squeeze it out.) Add some more olive oil to the pan with the mushrooms and some balsamic vinegar–about twice as much oil as vinegar. Grind in some black pepper. Warm lightly, pour over greens and garnish with pecans.

*I don't mean to give you the impression that I have the most discriminating taste buds. Usually, I can only tell OK from horrible, but in this case, I like the sea salt that my friends Fred and Karen sent me from Hawaii. You're going to have to find your own sea salt. Fred and Karen can't send it to everybody....

Don't wear shoes that hurt your feet.

Washboard Stomach

We live in a culture that worships a washboard stomach. This is sick. Think about it. Would you really want to be close to someone who spent all their free time working to make their stomach look like they move cement block for a living? I say find someone who actually lays block. They'd probably be a lot more interesting, and they'd be able to drink beer in their free time, because they already had the ab thing under control. I used to have a flat stomach. I got over it. I had kids and no matter what I did, or how little I weighed, there was still that little pouch of flab....

Remember Twiggy? Remember when we thought Twiggy (the fashion model from the 60s or 70s) was really sick looking? Look at her now. Compared to most models, she looks over-weight. Examine very closely, say, the Victoria's Secret Catalog. (Your husband will be happy to help you with this research.) Put a piece of black electrical tape over the breasts of the models, because no matter how much you vomit, silicone doesn't lose weight. Now look. These are women who must dedicate their lives to starvation. They could have been electrical engineers or astronauts or gifted, blessed chefs, but no! They chose to be icky, skinny models. Would you want one of these women for *your* mother? Of course not!

Roasted Beet Salad

8–10 medium beets
3 tablespoons balsamic vinegar
3 tablespoons olive oil
½ cup chopped roasted walnuts
⅓ cup crumbled Roquefort cheese
freshly ground black pepper

Wash the beets and trim the stems and roots. Put them in an ovenproof pan and roast at 400° until you can pierce them easily with a fork. This will vary depending on the size of the beets, but check after 20 minutes. Cool, peel the beets and cut into julienne. (Jim! Julienne means sticks a little thicker than a wooden matchstick!) Toss the beets with the vinegar and oil. Cover and chill until serving time. Serve with walnuts and cheese on top. Grind pepper over everything. You might also want to serve this on a base of intense flavored greens like arugula or watercress. If you can't do the cheese thing, or the walnuts, it would be okay—but not the same.

Your friends don't love you because
you have thin upper arms.

Even as an adult, there may be a part of you that hates eating beets. (It is probably the same part that hates eating soap.) That's because the awful canned vegetable they tried to force down our throats as kids tasted like Ivory. This recipe is the beet's chance at redemption. It's good any time of year you can find fresh beets. You may also want to toast the nuts if you like walnuts with that extra deep flavor and crunch.

Red Bell Pepper Salad Dressing

½ chopped red bell pepper
4 cloves garlic
⅔ cup olive oil
⅓ cup wine vinegar
½ teaspoon basil
⅓ cup sugar
Fresh ground black pepper to taste

Put all in a blender and give it a buzz. Serve on greens.

I made this by accident one day. I didn't mean to put in ⅓ cup of sugar, but it was good.

It's perfect with fresh leaf lettuce from the garden.

Exercising

When I was younger, I could stay skinny with no exercise. Actually, I did some light weight lifting—I repeatedly raised 3.5 ounce Snickers bars to my lips. As I got older, it's been harder, but do any of us really want to weigh what we did when we were twenty? People might get us mixed up with twenty-year-olds all the time. They'd say, "She looks *exactly* like that college sophomore, except she's all wrinkly and has gray hair." I started a regular exercise program anyway. These are my tips for success:

1. Exercise in the morning whenever possible so you can feel virtuous all day. If you are running or walking and people pass you in their cars, think less of them, it will raise your self esteem.

2. If you miss a day, don't beat yourself up. Count your successes, not your failures. Think of your rest days as proof that you are not a type A personality.

3. When you are running, imagine Lyle Lovett is just a couple of strides ahead of you. OK. Maybe this visualization won't work for everybody....

SALADS

Sun-Dried Tomato Vinaigrette

¼ cup balsamic vinegar
¼ cup sun-dried tomatoes, minced
2 tablespoons olive oil
2 tablespoons water
1 tablespoon fresh chopped tarragon, or 1 teaspoon
 dried tarragon
1 tablespoon Dijon mustard
1 teaspoon sugar

Place all in a jar and shake well. Shake well before serving.

This recipe gives you one more reason not to buy salad dressing in the bottle, because while they are not all downright disgusting, you have to admit there is an awful lot of stuff in there that you have no idea where it came from. Make this instead; you'll feel better about that whole multi-syllabic food-ingredient issue.

SALADS 37

Soups

A Little Lunch's Tomato Bisque

¾ cup chopped onions
⅔ cup butter*
¾ teaspoon dill seed
1 teaspoon dill weed
1 teaspoon oregano
¼ cup flour
3 cups chicken stock
3–4 cups canned tomatoes, chopped
1½ teaspoons salt
½ teaspoon pepper
¼ cup chopped parsley
¼ cup honey
1 cup cream*
½ cup half and half

A very long time ago, back when Savories of Stillwater, Minnesota (a great restaurant), was called A Little Lunch, they published the tomato bisque recipe in the paper. Aren't you glad I wrote it down? However, it is a little rich. If your objective is to kill yourself with a slow cardiac stranglehold, make it this way. If not, tone it down with 2 tablespoons olive oil instead of ⅔ cup butter, and use milk or half and half for the cream. Even I have to draw the line somewhere... and some of you didn't even think I had a line. Shame on you!

Sauté onions in oil or butter with dill and oregano. Add flour and stir to make a roux. (A roux is fat and flour cooked together as a base for thickening a liquid. It's pronounced roo, like the character in *Winnie the Pooh*.) Slowly stir in warm stock—then it won't get lumpy. Add tomatoes, salt and pepper. Simmer 15 minutes. Add parsley, honey and your choice of dairy product. Heat, do not boil.

*look for the light version on the right.

Southeast Asian Curried Soup

3 tablespoons oil
1 large onion, diced
2 large garlic cloves, minced
2 teaspoons grated peeled fresh ginger root
1 teaspoon salt
2 cups water
1 teaspoon each coriander, cumin and turmeric
1 teaspoon crushed dried chilies
15 blanched almonds, ground
2 bay leaves
14 oz. can coconut milk
4 cups peeled and cubed pie pumpkin,
  winter squash or carrots
2–3 cups chopped fresh kale, spinach or chard
fresh lime or lemon juice
toasted shredded coconut

This weird soup has become a family favorite. There was a time when it would have surprised me to hear the boys say, "Mom, make that soup with the squash and spinach," but not anymore.

Sauté onion and garlic in oil. Add ginger and salt and continue to sauté until onions are translucent. Add water, spices and nuts and simmer for 5 minutes. Add bay leaves, coconut milk and pumpkin and simmer gently, uncovered, for about 40 minutes until pumpkin is tender. Remove bay leaves and put soup in the blender. Lightly blend. Put back in pan over medium heat. Stir in greens and cook a few minutes until tender. Remove pot from heat and squeeze in lemon or lime juice to taste, garnish with toasted coconut and serve.

Cabbage Borscht

8 cups water
1 pound beef soup meat and bone*
2 teaspoons salt
1 onion, chopped
½ cup sugar
1 medium cabbage, cut up
1 large can whole tomatoes
½ teaspoon sour salt (confession, I have never used this)
½ cup ketchup

Place all ingredients in pot and cook until meat is tender. Isn't that easy?

***Vegetarian version: Saute 2 large coarsely chopped portabella mushrooms and a few shiitakes. Substitute them for the beef. Add dark miso paste to taste. (A couple of tablespoons, probably.)**

One summer I taught horseback riding at Camp Butwin, run by the St. Paul Jewish Community Center. This was just one experience that contributed to my richly confused spiritual background. It may be the reason my friend Steve Minkowski thought I was indeed a Jewish princess who was switched in the hospital nursery and mistakenly sent home with a nice Methodist couple. Think about it. It could explain a lot. At any rate, I'd like to thank Bill and Mona for raising me. I'll thank my real parents, Bernie and Irene, for my tastebuds and Sid's wife for this recipe.

Apricot and Lentil Soup

3 tablespoons olive oil
1 large onion, finely chopped
2 large cloves garlic, minced
⅔ cup dried apricots, chopped
1½ cups red lentils, well rinsed
5 cups chicken or veggie broth
3 tablespoons soy sauce
3 Roma tomatoes, peeled, seeded and chopped, or their
   canned equivalent
1 teaspoon each ground cumin, dried thyme, salt and pepper
¼ cup fresh lemon juice
¾ cup fresh cilantro leaves, chopped

Sauté onion, garlic and apricots in oil about 12 minutes, until onion is tender. Add lentils, broth and soy sauce, bring to a boil. Reduce heat and simmer, covered, about 30 minutes or until lentils are tender. Stir in tomatoes, cumin, thyme, salt and pepper. Simmer, covered, 10 minutes longer. In food processor, blend half of soup until smooth. Return puree to the soup pot. Stir in lemon juice and salt and pepper to taste. Serve sprinkled with cilantro.

This recipe is a favorite at my almost annual "Longest Night" party. I live in Minnesota, in case you haven't picked up on it by now. On December 21st, my family and friends gather for a bonfire where we burn vacation brochures that have pictures of beaches on them. Another mid-winter event we like is the "Go Tropo" party where people come in swimsuits or resort wear and those white felt bunny boots that are so popular with Minnesotans. However, the older we get, the less attractive we are in bunny boots, don't you think? (I wouldn't serve this soup at the "Go Tropo" party, though; it doesn't look good with a paper umbrella in it.)

Anne's Cheese Carrot Soup

2 tablespoons butter
½ cup chopped onion
1 lb. chopped carrots
1 lb. peeled, cubed potatoes
6 cups chicken or vegetable broth
½ teaspoon thyme
bay leaf
⅛ teaspoon tabasco
½ teaspoon Worcestershire sauce
½ teaspoon sugar
1½ cups milk
1–2 cups grated cheddar cheese

Melt butter in a heavy, large pan and sauté onions until golden. Add carrots, potatoes, broth, thyme and bay leaf. Simmer until carrots are tender. Remove bay leaf. Puree soup in blender until smooth. Return to pot. Add remaining ingredients and stir over low heat until cheese is melted.

Go back to doing what you were doing
before you started twitching.

This recipe came from Anne Andersen, teacher extraordinaire. I like it because it uses up carrots and it tastes cheesy without being all cheese.

Tropical Crab Soup

½ cup butter
½ onion, diced small
⅛ teaspoon garlic, minced
¾ cup flour
2 cups coconut milk, warmed
2 cups half and half, warmed
12 oz. king crab meat, diced medium
2 cups chopped spinach
1 teaspoon chicken bouillon
¼ teaspoon ground white pepper

In a thick bottomed soup pot, sauté onion in butter on medium until transparent. Add garlic. Sauté, but do not brown. Take pan off heat. Stir in flour till smooth. Put back on heat and cook on medium for 10 minutes, constantly stirring. Do not brown. Take off heat. Add warm coconut milk. Put back on heat and simmer, stirring. Add warm half and half. Simmer for 30 minutes, stirring. Add crab meat, spinach and chicken bouillon to taste. Simmer 5 minutes. Season with pepper.

No one else really cares about your hairdo.

I had a soup like this at a restaurant when I lived in Hawaii. It was so good I asked for the recipe, but I had to change it because you can't get all the stuff on the mainland. The original recipe called for taro leaves. They were to be blanched for 20 minutes. I was sure this was a mistake that would rob the poor taro of its wonderful nutrients. I just chopped them up and threw them in. Later, as we were eating the soup, I felt my throat closing off. It became itchy and kind of hard to breathe. I later learned from a neighbor (who attempted to put taro in her salad and barely made it to the hospital—which was next door to her house) that it makes your throat swell shut if it's not cooked enough. Oh, well. So much for reading the directions. I'm not putting taro in this soup because it doesn't grow in Minnesota, does it? It grows in places where your skin doesn't crack in the winter.

Deliciously Wonderful Garlic Soup

olive oil
4 heads (not cloves) garlic, peeled and chopped
6 large carrots, peeled and sliced
½ large onion, chopped
3 medium potatoes, peeled and cubed
2–3 cups chicken or vegetable broth
¼ teaspoon ground mace
½ teaspoon thyme
1 teaspoon salt

Heat a little olive oil in a large heavy saucepan. Add garlic and gently sauté until golden brown. Remove garlic from pan and save. Add carrots and a little more oil to the pan and sauté on medium-high heat until carrots caramelize (turn medium brown in spots). Add the onions and continue to sauté until limp. Add potatoes, broth, spices and salt. The liquid should cover the vegetables. Bring to a boil, lower the heat and cover. Simmer until the potatoes are very soft. (Maybe 20–30 minutes; it's not critical. Just stir it now and then and keep the heat low so it doesn't burn.) Remove from heat and transfer the contents of the pan and the reserved garlic to the blender. Blend it all up till very smooth. Return to the pan. Add more water if it is too thick—but you want it to be a thick creamy soup. Gently warm and serve.

This soup was inspired by the roasted garlic soup they serve at Cafe Zander in St. Paul—a wonderful restaurant in every way. Like their soup, it will probably make you smell of garlic for three days, but don't let that stop you. Just make sure you keep the sheets real tight around your neck the first night after you eat it. I think this soup is perfect served with Lisa's Prune bread. Also (I can't stop! This has never happened to me before!) this recipe is accidentally quite acceptable to serve to your vegetarian, lowfat, non-dairy, non-wheat-eating, non-sugar-eating, whatever-else-friends, if they're still walking among the emotionally stable.... (Don't give them the bread though.)

North African Chicken Soup

4 cans no-fat chicken broth
2 lemons, juice only from one, one cut in wedges
2 small turnips and 2 carrots, peeled and chopped
3 onions, 2 chopped, one stuck with 2 whole cloves
1 bunch parsley, chopped
2 teaspoons salt
½ teaspoon pepper
1 teaspoon cinnamon and 1 teaspoon chili powder
¼ teaspoon powdered saffron or turmeric
1 lb. cooked chicken meat, cubed
2 eggs

Put all ingredients except chicken, eggs and lemon wedges in a large pot and simmer until vegetables are tender. Add chicken pieces. Stir 1 cup of soup into 2 beaten eggs. Return mixture to soup pot and stir. Reheat, but don't boil. Serve hot with lemon wedges for squeezing into soup.

I used to help teach a cooking class for John's school when he was in fifth grade. What was I thinking?! Those kids were nuts; but this soup is surprisingly interesting and comforting at the same time, and you can make it amazingly quickly if you have some leftover chicken meat and broth.

46 / SOUPS

Edie

Rest your suspicious mind.
This is okay.
So she likes to suck the babies' toes.
Put their tiny digits in her mouth
and caress them with her tongue.
Don't worry.
The newspaper doesn't need to
get hold of this,
But.
Also.
She kisses
Their wrinkly little heels and soles,
And blows fat trumpet sounds
On their tummies
Until they squirm and squeal.

It's her job.
She walks quietly every morning
To the garden,
Gently peels back the cabbage leaves,
Revealing fresh babies
Curled inside.
She wipes the dew from their brows and
Wraps them in soft flannel
Carefully contemplating
Their little
Baby
Noses

SOUPS 47

Potty Training

My nephew, Jake, who is now in medical school, made me laugh when he was little. I was baby-sitting and he was about three. He had to go to the bathroom, so I put him on the toilet. He looked at me and said in a very urgent, pleading voice, "Ohee eye ee pie ee!"

"What, Jakey?" I said.

He repeated, "Ohee eye ee pie ee!"

"Jakey, I can't understand you," I said with frustration. We repeated ourselves many times, until his older sister Jessie, 4, walked up and said in her characteristic deadpan, "He said, 'Lori, I need privacy.'"

Right.

Cold Orange Beet Soup

8 beets, peeled and cut into ½" dice
⅓ cup chopped red onion
2 cups no-fat chicken stock
2 cups water
1½ cups fresh orange juice
grated zest of 2 oranges—better get organic ones
2 tablespoons sugar
2 tablespoons red wine vinegar
1 cup heavy cream
salt and pepper

Place the beets, onions, stock and water in a large saucepan. Heat to boiling. Reduce heat and simmer uncovered until the beets are very tender, about 30 minutes. Remove from heat and stir in the orange juice and zest. Let cool to room temperature. Stir in the sugar. Puree the soup in a blender until smooth and pour into a bowl. Stir in the vinegar, cream and salt and pepper to taste. Refrigerate until cold. Serve the soup cold with a little garnish of sour cream or whipped cream.

This is probably my favorite soup recipe in the whole wide world. (Don't you just love that expression, whole wide world? It sounds like something a little kid would say.) Even if you think you don't like beets, you should try this soup. If you are my brother Jim, who is weird about cold soup, you should start eating this soup hot. Eat it very slowly, so it is cold by the time you are finishing. Now see if that was so bad.

She Will Lift You Up on Eagle's Wings

Some conversations are unusual. No matter how much you like to talk, it's better to just listen.

"Lori," Nancy began, "I'm going to have to give you your Christmas present early this year. I was going to give you five chickens, but they're getting too old. I got six roosters in the dozen chicks I ordered this spring and I really only need one. Six roosters is five too many; they're starting to fight with each other, and they all crow at one time, so if you want to come over some morning this week we'll kill them."

Nancy is a vegetarian.

I've only killed one thing in my life that was bigger than a mosquito, and it was with my car.

On the prescribed morning, Nancy and I walked across the dewy lawn to the chicken coop. We hid the instruments of destruction behind our backs: the ax, knives, buckets and such. Nancy pulled a chunk of tree stump out onto the grass and drove two large nails into it, a couple of inches apart. Then she drove another nail into a standing tree and attached a piece of clothes-line cord. Next she walked into the chicken coop.

"Come here, little chicken," she crooned, scooping up a rust red rooster with a brilliant comb. "Nice chickie," she continued, stroking the poor doomed fowl. "You're going to a new life now, it's OK, don't worry. It will all be over in a minute and you'll be in a better place." Nancy, I suspect, really believed this was true for the bird. She meditates and reads a lot, studying the religions of the world, especially those of the Far East.

The chicken, however, was doubtful. I don't think the chicken even read the stuff the Jehovah's Witness people bring around.

I'd like to describe, in detail, the next part, but I couldn't look. I know that Nancy put the chicken's head between the nails on the stump and held its feet. I heard the ax whacking away, and the rooster protesting this act of animal sexual discrimination. I heard the thunk as the body hit the five gallon bucket that kept it from running around spewing blood. I waited for the flopping to stop and I stepped up to do my part.

First, I dipped the carcass in a large pot of boiling water. Grabbing the chicken by the feet, I then strung it up to the tree, what used to be head end down. I ripped the feathers out with a fury and tossed them in the wheelbarrow as Nancy seduced her next victim. Nothing will keep your mind on the business of plucking chickens like not wanting to watch what's going on ten feet away. I plucked with a giftedness I never knew I had.

When I had five naked chickens in my bowl, we carried them over to the picnic table. The evisceration was more of a science project. We studied the livers, kidneys, heart and gullets. We cut off the feet and pulled the tendons to make them move. We were just a smidge away from that guy who made lamp shades out of people, only these were chickens, and they were quickly becoming lunch. When the designated portion of the flock were cleaned, cut up and bagged, we went back to the scene of the crime. Tossing stray heads in the wheelbarrow with the feathers and innards, Nancy resumed her mantra. "It's all over, little chickens. You're going to a new life now," she said as she dug a hole in the back field and buried the evidence.

Chicken Stock

This is the way I make chicken stock. I usually buy whole chickens from my co-op or local chicken farmer. I really think natural chicken tastes better and after just 5 minutes of a public radio report on what they feed to chickens, even Dick the Skeptic wanted the kids to stop eating chicken at the college lunch line. The effort it takes to find good chicken is worth it.

OK. I was going to be talking about chicken stock.... If I'm cutting up my whole chickens, I throw the backs and necks in a freezer bag and forget about them. If I roast a chicken and have bones left over, I add them to the bag. Then, when stuff starts falling on my head when I open the freezer door, due to the large quantity of chicken parts, I make stock.

Take a big roaster pan, the kind that can go in the oven or on the stove and put all the chicken in it. Put it in the oven at 400° and roast until things start to get nice and brown. You don't even have to thaw the chicken out. Don't burn it, because burned food tastes bitter, but let it get caramel brown.

Next, put the bones, with the meat attached, of course, in a big stock pot. (It's worth having a nice stainless steel stock pot with a heavy bottom. You'll find you use it all the time.) Pour off the fat that is in the roaster pan and throw it away, give it to the dog, or use it instead of butter on your mashed potatoes. Mmmmm.

Add a few cups of water to the roaster and heat it on the stove, stirring, until the sticky bits come off the bottom, cleaning the pan. Pour that mixture into the stock pot and add more water to cover the bones.

At this point, you have to think what you're going to do with the stock. If you want a generic stock that you can freeze and use for a million things, put a little garlic and onion in the pot, maybe some celery, parsley, peppercorns and a little salt. It doesn't matter that much, because usually when you need chicken stock in a recipe, you're going to season some more.

Simmer for an hour or two with the lid on the pan, taste it and if you want more intense flavor, cook it with the lid off. Strain the stock and chill the liquid. Take any fat off the top when it's cold. Cool the bones and pick the meat off of them to use in soup.

Breads

Almond Cardamom Popovers

1 cup skim milk
¾ teaspoon ground cardamom
dash salt
1 teaspoon almond extract
1 egg
2 egg whites
1 tablespoon unsalted butter, melted
1 cup all purpose flour
Topping:
1 tablespoon unsalted butter, melted
1 tablespoon sugar

I really like this recipe. It came from the folks at *Cooking Pleasures Magazine*. I would recommend that you join their cooking club. It provides you with the magazine as one of the many perks—they have good recipes.

In large bowl, combine milk, cardamom, salt, almond extract, egg and egg whites; mix with wire whisk until combined. Whisk in 1 tablespoon melted butter. Add flour; whisk just until smooth. DO NOT OVERBEAT. Let batter rest 30 minutes.

Meanwhile, place oven rack in lower third of oven; heat to 325°. Spray 5 cups in popover pan with nonstick cooking spray. Pour batter into sprayed cups. Place on rack in lower third of oven; immediately increase oven temperature to 425°. Bake 20 minutes. Reduce oven temperature to 325°; bake an additional 20 minutes or until golden brown and firm. Make a 1" slit in side of each popover with sharp knife; bake an additional 5 minutes. Remove from oven; brush tops with 1 tablespoon melted butter. Sprinkle with sugar. Serve warm.

Note: It is worth buying a popover pan for this recipe.

Early Morning Meditation

This is the sound of the stream
rounding the bend
Where velvet moss blankets the
stump
And grape vine touches the water.

This is the sound of the scarlet
bird
At the tip of the tree
Where branches etch the blue sky.

This is the sound of the dew drop
That falls from the blade of grass
Next to the nodding purple wild
geranium.

This is the sound of the ruffed
grouse,
And the dog's warm breath,
As she walks beside me.

This is the long line of sound,
As two squirrels chase
Through the dry leaves of the
maple woods.

Shirley's Biscuits

1 cup self-rising flour
½ cup cake flour
½ teaspoon baking powder
¼ teaspoon salt
1 tablespoon sugar
3 tablespoons shortening
¾ cup buttermilk
¼ cup cream
½ cup additional flour

Sift the dry ingredients together, cut in the shortening and stir in the wet ingredients. Put ½ cup of additional flour in a small bowl. Use an ice cream scoop to scoop out portions of dough. Drop the dough in the flour to coat it—it will be too wet to handle without the coating of flour. Put the blobs in a greased 8x8" pan, kind of "snuggled up against each other" as Shirley would say. Bake at 475° for 15–18 minutes. Makes about 9 smallish biscuits. Serve warm with butter and jam.

I heard Shirley Corriher speak at "Food on Film," a food styling convention I used to go to. She is a wild and fun woman who's a food chemist and can make a person who thought that wood was one of the elements (me) actually care about a starch molecule's romantic attraction to water and how this union will produce a flaky pie crust. Shirley has a book out called *CookWise*, and I know that if Santa brings it to you, you will love it as much as I do. That is, if you really care about food and wonder why it does what it does. This is a recipe for biscuits she gave on the radio. They are truly light and heavenly. It's almost like each one of them had its own little angel lounging around on top of it.

Apple Cranberry Spa Muffins

1 cup all purpose flour
½ cup oats
1 teaspoon baking powder
1 teaspoon cinnamon
¼ teaspoon salt
¾ cup chopped apple
¾ cup dried cranberries
¼ cup currants
¾ cup maple syrup
¼ cup canola oil
1 teaspoon vanilla

Preheat oven to 375°. Mix dry ingredients together. Stir in fruit, then wet ingredients. Bake in paper lined muffin tins for 12–15 minutes.

Some pets are from other planets.

Dorothy Deetz, mother, wife, massage therapist, computer wizard and rescue queen smuggled this recipe out of a famous spa where they charge people to be soaked with fire hoses. (Isn't life funny?) Dorothy always makes these when the Moms get together to have complete thoughts.

Reed's Hot Cakes

2 eggs
2 cups buttermilk
1½ tablespoons sugar
2 tablespoons oil
1¾ cup flour
1 teaspoon salt
1 teaspoon baking soda
1 teaspoon baking powder

Mix it all together. Heat a griddle and lightly butter. Pour some batter on the griddle and turn over when the surface of the pancake is covered with bubbles. You know how to do this. You can make this batter the night before and keep it in the fridge. Of course, you need to serve these with real maple syrup.

Never buy cheap underwear.

I spent many of my formative years working at Reed's Drug and Department Store in beautiful downtown Stillwater, Minnesota. This was in the days when you could still buy a roll of masking tape on Main Street. My first station at Reed's was in the soda fountain where Baya, the cook, would go on *Reed's Time to Trade Radio Show* every day and read the lunch special, "...for number three we have the hot roast beef sandwich, mashed potatoes, gravy and coffee. For number four we have the boiled dinner..." Meanwhile, the dish washer blasted the leftovers down the disposal with the power sprayer and practiced her dream of becoming a country western singer. They had a good recipe for hot cakes.

Oatmeal Pumpkin Bread

3 cups flour
1 cup uncooked regular oats
1 tablespoon plus 1 teaspoon baking powder
2 teaspoons ground cinnamon
1 teaspoon baking soda
¼ teaspoon salt
1 teaspoon ground ginger
½ teaspoon ground nutmeg or mace
¼ teaspoon ground cloves (optional)
1 cup honey
½ cup vegetable oil
4 eggs, or egg substitute
⅔ cup unsweetened orange juice
16 oz. can pumpkin
½ to 1 cup walnuts or pecans, chopped

Combine first 9 ingredients in a large bowl. Combine honey, oil and eggs; add to flour mixture, stirring just until blended. Stir in orange juice, pumpkin and walnuts. Spoon batter into 2 large (8½ x 4½ x 3") pans or 3 small loafpans. Char likes using 3 smaller bread pans that have been coated with cooking spray. Bake at 350° for 1 hour or until a wooden pick inserted in center comes out clean. Cool in pans 10 minutes, remove from pans and let cool completely on wire racks.

Remember my friend Charlotte, the dietitian and opera singer? Now we have to add Peace Corp Volunteer to the list. She is currently in Mongolia, so I don't know how I will get this book to her, unless I try to e-mail it, and that would be beyond my computer capabilities. Anyway—Char gave me this recipe, and if Char says it's good, it's good. And Char, I'm sorry I gave you a hard time when you told me how cold it was in Mongolia in centigrade, and I said that wasn't really that cold. I'm sure by now you have experienced the true cold with which we are so intimately familiar here in Minnesota. If you're huddled in a yurt drinking fermented mare's milk and eating sheep intestines, what difference does it make if it's -25°C or F?

Lana's Scones

2 cups flour
2 tablespoons sugar
2 teaspoons baking powder
½ teaspoon baking soda
½ teaspoon salt
½ cup melted butter or oil
⅔ cup buttermilk

Mix dry ingredients. Stir in butter and buttermilk. Add any additions. Knead briefly. Pat out into a circle about 10" across. Cut like a pie into 8 pieces. Sprinkle top with something appropriate, like sugar. Bake on lightly greased baking sheet at 425° for 14–16 minutes.

Additions: chocolate chips or chunks, white or dark; raisins, dried cranberries, nuts, blueberries. For savory scones—a lunchbox favorite—add cheddar cheese, chopped ham, chives, etc. Sprinkle them with some additional cheese.

Lana Olin gave me this recipe for scones. I changed it a little, but not much. It is excellent. If you keep buttermilk powder around, you can even make these when you don't have buttermilk.

Banana Bread

1 cup sugar or ⅔ cup honey
½ cup butter or oil
2 eggs
4 tablespoons buttermilk
3 bananas, mashed
1 teaspoon baking soda
1 cup whole wheat flour
1 cup white or whole wheat flour
½ teaspoon salt

Beat sugar, oil and eggs together. Stir in bananas and buttermilk. Mix dry ingredients and stir into batter. Bake in a greased loaf pan at 350° for 60 minutes, or until wooden pick PLUNGED into it's very heart comes out clean, not gooey.

Usually older is wiser, but occasionally older is just lumpier.

I think banana bread is better made with whole wheat flour because it stays moister. Try it and see; I just might be right.

Doughnut Holes

2 cups flour
¼ cup sugar
3 teaspoons baking powder
1 teaspoon salt
½ teaspoon nutmeg
½ teaspoon mace
¼ cup vegetable oil
¾ cup milk
1 egg
oil for deep fat frying

I don't think we eat nearly enough fried food these days.

Mix dry ingredients. Add oil, milk and egg. Mix well with a fork. Drop by teaspoons into hot oil (375°). Fry about 3 minutes or until golden. Drain on paper towels. Roll warm doughnut holes in cinnamon sugar or powdered sugar. Makes 2½ dozen.

Happy Hour

A time when everyone else is crazy,
And when I am perfectly sane,
And they panic their way through another hour,
And I...I eat some toast.
I sit back in this toast-eating-
happy-hour,
Sectioned off from the rest of time,
Sectioned off by those mysterious powers of toast that science will never fully understand,
And I hear only my own toastly crunchings,
And I smell only burned bread and cinnamon,
But I see the world continuing outside of my bubble of toast-
induced happiness,
And everyone is driving
themselves crazy.
They are worried, frantic, and toastless.
They aren't like me, with my entire hour of happiness brought by just
a piece of bread burned to
perfection.
But it seems that the hour
is over as soon as it has begun.
And my toast is gone.
And there are crazy people
all over the place.

John Gordon

My son, John, wrote this in tenth grade English class. I'm including it because toast is important.

Oatmeal Bread

2 cups rolled oats
2 cups boiling water
1 tablespoon oil
Mix and let cool.

1 tablespoon yeast
½ cup milk, warm
Dissolve yeast in milk.

½ cup sugar
1 teaspoon molasses
1 cup flour
Add to cooled oat mixture with yeast mixture. Beat well, cover with damp towel and let rise until double.

1½ teaspoons salt
3 cups flour—white or whole wheat work
Add to dough and knead until smooth and elastic, 10–15 minutes. Cover and let rise until double. Form into loaves. Put in 2 well-greased loaf pans. Let rise again in pan. Bake at 350° for 40 minutes.

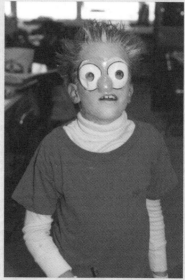

This is my current favorite yeast bread.

Lisa's Prune Bread

1¼ cups warm water
1 tablespoon butter
1 cup pitted prunes, quartered
1½ cups unbleached white flour
1½ cups whole wheat flour
2 tablespoons nonfat dry milk
3 tablespoons brown sugar
1 teaspoon fennel seed
1 teaspoon salt
2 teaspoons yeast
½ cup chopped walnuts

Place all ingredients except the walnuts in the machine as directed for your model. Set for white bread, 2 lb. loaf. Add walnuts when the beeper sounds. If you use the machine just to mix and rise the dough, punch it down, put in a greased bread pan or pie tin for a round loaf, let rise, and bake at 350° for about 35–40 minutes.

All whining should stop at age seven.

I was given a bread machine by a company that I worked for. They are actually very nice to have, especially if you just use them to make the dough and you bake the loaf in the oven. You get a much better crust that way. Kids probably love bread machine bread because it doesn't have much crust—and you surely know that crust is poisonous to children. Either that or they refuse to eat it so they can chew it into the shape of a gun and shoot their pacifist mother.

French Bread (Italian Style)

1 teaspoon yeast
2 cups water at 85°
1 teaspoon salt
6 cups unbleached bread flour

Dissolve yeast in the water. Add salt and flour until you can't stir in anymore. Knead in the rest of the flour, or what the dough will take. It should make a smooth elastic dough that feels like a baby's butt. Put it in a large bowl and cover the bowl with plastic. Now you can either leave the bowl out at room temperature for 6–8 hours or put it in the refrigerator for 24 hours. When the time is up, turn the dough out on a floured surface. DON'T PUNCH IT DOWN. Divide the dough in half and gently roll each half into a ball. Let it sit and rest for ½ hour. Now gently form the dough into a longish loaf, like a fat loaf of French bread. Use lots of flour on the work surface so it doesn't stick. Be careful again not to punch the air out of it. Slash the tops of the loaves every inch or two—I just use a scissors.

Preheat the oven to 425°. If you have a baking stone, let it preheat with the oven. If you also own a bread peel, let the loaves rise on a surface that has been sprinkled with cornmeal so they don't stick. If you don't have a bread peel, (it's a thin, wooden, ping pong paddle-looking thing that slips bread and pizza in and out of ovens), let the loaves rise on a cookie sheet with no rim (or the back of a cookie sheet), that is covered with corn meal. Otherwise, put them right on a baking sheet that is

I learned to make this French Bread from George Formaro of the South Union Bakery in Des Moines, Iowa. (Mmmmm.) His mom came from Sicily and he spent his life trying to figure out how to make bread like hers. You would think he would have just asked her, wouldn't you? Unless you have teenage sons, and then you know that he no longer believes she knows anything. (Actually, George later told me he tried to learn from his mom, but she threw in this and that and never had a recipe— Sicilians, you gotta love 'em.) This makes a yeasty, crusty, moist bread with big holes inside that couldn't be any better in my estimation. (Well, it was better when we ate it with little hunks of imported chocolate stuffed into the bread and smeared it with unsalted butter.)

greased and covered with cornmeal. Lightly cover the loaves and let rise for 1½ hours or until they hold a finger poke mark when you press on the dough. Uncover and carefully slide them to the baking stone with the bread peel or cookie sheet, or put the whole prepared baking sheet in the oven and bake 35 minutes or until the internal temperature of the loaf is 208°.

Notes: You don't need to cover the loaves during the final rising if your kitchen is humid. You just don't want the outside of the dough to dry out and not be stretchy enough to rise anymore—which can happen with dry, cool Minnesota winters.

An instant read thermometer will cost you $10.00–$15.00 and is an invaluable tool. It is especially wonderful for checking the temperature when grilling such things as fish.

If your house smells bad, check the garbage and the cat box.

New Swimsuit

I took my swimsuit on vacation and somehow left it there. I hope for its sake a great looking Polynesian woman found it and is now walking the beach with her long black hair swinging in the tropical breeze.

The suit never had a shot at the cover of *Conte Nast* when it belonged to me.

I thought I could get by without a swimsuit, but you can swim naked at the state park beach near my house just so many times before the ranger folds a park map into a paper airplane and sails a note over suggesting you're scaring the campers.

Realizing I needed something, I found an old yellow one piece in the bottom drawer of my dresser. I hadn't had it on in years but there are photographs of me wearing it near the end of last century. OK, in the shots, I'm pretty far in the distance and there's a lot of minimizing ocean around, but I think I look pretty petite in that suit. Svelte almost.

Why a rolled rib roast came to mind when I tried it on this time, I have no idea. It must not have been a quality garment. The fabric seemed to have atrophied from lack of use. Shrunk in the drawer like calf muscles under the cast on a broken leg. Sad.

Not to be discouraged, I zipped out to find a new one. Since the summer was half over, the swimwear was cheap. Last season's styles would be fine. I knew a dark color is usually flatter-ing, and even though they had some of those geriatric bikinis with the long tops and high bottoms, there isn't much between my neck and knees that anybody could stand to look at, so I chose all tank styles.

They must buy the lights for fitting rooms at animal laboratory salvage stores. The harsh glare is perfect if you're there to dissect small mammals. It makes you look like something you'd find under a rock and save to use for fishing.

The mirrors are kind of close, too. Not much looks good at twelve inches, especially thighs. For me, a quarter of a mile is ideal. And, not to be disparaging of any ethnic group, but white women are best covered up. I've never seen a *National Geographic* article with beautiful pictures of naked, middle-aged white women. If a kid kept an issue like that under the mattress, it would give him nightmares.

I tried suit after suit. I looked from the front. I turned sideways and sucked in my stomach, then looked over my shoulder at the rear view. Given I'm pretty flat chested, I couldn't figure how I managed to produce back boobs bigger than the ones I have on the front. I longed to go back to the figure of my youth, but remembered that wasn't so hot either.

So, I stood there in the fitting room of Marshall's Discount Store and tried to love my puckery stomach. I stared in the mirror and attempted saggy breast worship. I thought of my substantial upper arms as strong and healthy, my thighs as muscular and powerful.

I was starting to tear up a little when I heard a knock on the door.

"Are you OK, ma'am?" came the voice of the fitting room attendant.

"Yeah," I said. "I'm fine."

"Can I get anything for you?"

"You want to put these back?" I asked, giving her the rejects and hanging on to a nice black suit that met my goal of not being horrible. Also, I figured, it would look a lot better if I took off the bumper tennis shoes and crew socks.

Tropical Fruit Bread

¾ cup water
6 tablespoons milk
3 tablespoons oil
3 tablespoons sugar
½ teaspoon ground ginger
½ teaspoon nutmeg
¾ teaspoon salt
1 cup whole wheat flour
2 cups bread flour
2¼ teaspoons yeast
½ cup diced dried sugared pineapple
¼ cup diced dried mango (optional)
6 tablespoons grated coconut
6 tablespoons chopped macadamia nuts

This is wonderful, moist bread, but it has to bake a little longer to be done in the center. You may have to set the crust control on dark if you find your bread machine doesn't bake it consistently. If you bake it in the oven, in a round loaf, you'll have better control.

Put all but last three ingredients in bread pan in the order recommended by your bread machine maker. Add about half the pineapple, which will be cut into bits by the kneading. Set for white bread, medium crust. Press start. Add remaining pineapple, mango, coconut and nuts at beeper or after first kneading. Again, if you just use the machine to mix the dough, bake as directed for prune bread (pg. 65).

Odd looking people are usually more interesting.

Side Dishes

Linda's Veggies

fresh vegetables such as:
broccoli
cauliflower
carrots
bell peppers
mushrooms
onions
potatoes
olive oil
2 cloves garlic
½ teaspoon salt
2 tablespoons rice or balsamic vinegar

Clean and cut veggies into 1" chunks. Drizzle with olive oil. Roast in 500° oven for 15 minutes, or until firm veggies are tender. Toss with minced garlic, salt, vinegar and 2 tablespoons olive oil.

Tailgaters should be duct taped to the
bumpers of slow moving vehicles.

This is the way I cook vegetables most of the time. You can play with the dressing if you like—I usually use balsamic vinegar. You can add herbs too, but these are delicious.

Polenta with Peppers and Goat Cheese

Polenta:
7–8 cups cold water
2 cups coarse cornmeal (polenta)
¾ cup butter
1 cup freshly grated parmesan cheese
salt

Stir 7 cups cold water and the polenta together in a large heavy saucepan. Cook over low heat, stirring often and scraping the bottom of the pot, until thick and it no longer feels grainy on your tongue, about 30 minutes. Add more water if the polenta thickens too much before it's cooked. Stir in the butter and cheese and season to taste with the salt. Pour warm polenta into oiled jelly roll pan. Cover with plastic wrap. Cool until set.

Topping:
1 tablespoon olive oil
3 cloves garlic, sliced
1 green and 1 red bell pepper, sliced
2 tablespoons raisins
2 tablespoons dried sweet cherries
½ cup apple juice
fresh ground pepper
fresh goat cheese and grated parmesan for garnish

Sauté garlic and peppers over medium heat in olive oil, until peppers soften a bit, add rest of ingredients except cheeses and cook until the cider is reduced to half.

Slice the polenta into 4 x 5" pieces and grate some fresh parmesan on top. Put these on an ovenproof dish and broil until hot and toasty. Top with warm pepper mixture and a few dabs of goat cheese. Put back under the broiler until the cheese warms up.

I like polenta—Italian cooked cornmeal. It's easy, and you can make it the day ahead, if you like. Save it in a pan in the fridge and cut up the leftovers—if it's plain—and serve it for breakfast, warmed with maple syrup and vanilla yogurt on top. This polenta isn't plain, though. It was inspired by the pizza at Table of Contents in St. Paul, one of the best yup restaurants in the area. They recently changed their name to Red Fish Blue.

Risotto

Sauté about ¾ cup of chopped onions—don't measure—in a little butter over medium heat until onions are golden. In another pan warm about 5 cups of stock, chicken or vegetable is best. Add 1 cup of arborio rice to the onions and stir so the butter coats the rice. Add a little more butter if you like. (I also make this with olive oil.) We're only talking a couple of tablespoons of butter or oil. Add a ladle full of hot stock, stirring until the liquid is absorbed and add more stock. Keep this up, adding the stock about ½ cup at a time until the rice is al dente. This means tender, but not mushy to you non-Italians like me. The last bit of liquid should be ½ cup of white wine. Sometimes I have added 2 tablespoons brandy instead. It should be like rice in heavy cream. Remove from heat and stir in a handful of freshly grated—really, you don't want that stuff out of a can—parmesan cheese and one of these other additions if you like. The possibilities are endless:

some Gorgonzola cheese
smoked salmon or trout
sautéed mushrooms, especially porcini or shiitake
chopped procuitto ham

No kid goes to college with a pacifier.

I've seen recipes for risotto written by some pretty confused people. Risotto isn't just rice with stuff added to it. What makes it risotto is the way you cook the rice. First, you have to use arborio rice, which you get at a specialty food store. Then add hot broth to the rice and stir it constantly, until you have this wonderful, creamy mixture that is served and eaten immediately. Put a little piece of grilled fish next to it, or some steamed asparagus and you will have your diners in ecstasy. Really. But remember, timing is everything.

Sweet and Crunchy Couscous

1½ cups white grape juice
2 teaspoons oil
1 cup couscous—regular or whole wheat
1 cup mixed dried fruit, chopped, such as dates (yuck!),
   apricots, peaches, pears, etc.
¼ cup orange juice
1 teaspoon grated orange peel
¼ teaspoon each ground nutmeg and cinnamon
⅔ cup toasted chopped walnuts or pecans

**In large saucepan, combine grape juice and oil. Bring to a
boil, pour in couscous. Cover, remove from heat and let stand
5–10 minutes or until liquid is absorbed. Meanwhile, in small
saucepan over medium heat, combine fruit, orange juice,
orange peel and spices. Cover and simmer for 5 minutes. Gently
toss fruit mixture and nuts into couscous with a fork to keep
mixture fluffy. Serve warm or at room temperature.**

This recipe was one of the finalists
in a recipe contest. I was one of the
judges, so trust me. It was way better
than the millet ice cream. It's really
good and you can serve it at room
temperature, so you have less to do
at the last minute and you can have
another of Lisa's Margaritas.

California Pilaf

½ cup brown rice
¼ cup wild rice
¼ cup wheat berries—unground wheat, find it at the co-op
½ teaspoon aniseed
2¼ cups water
½ teaspoon salt

Simmer 30 minutes, covered. Remove from heat and let stand 15 minutes, covered, until liquid is absorbed.

1 tablespoon olive oil
2 green onions and 1 stalk celery, diced
1 green or red pepper, diced
4 shiitake mushrooms, chopped
1 clove garlic
1 teaspoon chili powder
½ teaspoon cumin

Sauté until onion is tender.

Add:

2 tablespoons pine nuts, toasted
2 tablespoons cilantro, chopped

The world would be a better place if there were no paper napkins.

I confess, I put this recipe in my late-eighties cookbook, but that is now sadly out of print and not even available at Half-Price Books. So I will do you the service of repeating it here. The idea for this recipe comes from a spa in California. Make it and you, too, will be rich, tanned, beautiful, and have a serious credit card debt problem.

Meyer's Lemon Pasta

¼ lb. bulk ground spicy pork sausage (optional)
3 Meyer's lemons
olive oil
4 cloves garlic
salt and pepper
1 tablespoon chopped fresh parsley
1 tablespoon chopped fresh chives
½ lb. linguini

Form the pork sausage into little meatballs and sauté until cooked through. Set aside. Cut the lemons into eighths, seed and remove the white part in the center. Including the peel, thinly slice over a bowl to catch the juices. Toss the lemon pieces in the bowl with the juice. Sauté the minced garlic cloves in a little olive oil. Add the lemons, salt and pepper to taste and herbs to the pan. Just warm gently. Cook the pasta, drain, season it with more olive oil and a little salt and pepper. Toss the pasta with the lemon mixture. Serve with a couple of meatballs and some fresh chives for garnish. Unlike my other recipes, which serve more, this is only for two.

Meyer's lemons are in season for a couple of months a year; I think it is in the winter. They are sweeter than most lemons and have a soft, mild rind that you can eat. My husband Dick eats the rinds of regular lemons, too. He also eats peanut shells. If you have a peanut shell eater in your life, I wouldn't waste the time making this delicious pasta for them. Their taste-buds are shot. However, make it for yourself, rent a good kissing movie and enjoy.

A Short Romantic Novel

There is something about going to Hawaii in the middle of the winter. You arrive at the Honolulu airport, the birds are singing, a gentle breeze floats through the windowless walkways, your nose stops bleeding.... After several days, you find yourself dressing in fabrics with large flowered prints and wearing a palm frond hat with a little bug dangling over the edge like a fish on a pole. You resolve to paint your dining room set hot pink, never to yell at your kids again and eat more papayas. But eventually, reluctantly, you must take the plane home. You board wearing your purple flip-flops and Hilo Hattie's aloha shirt, and you do not go into the bathroom to change when the plane reaches the North Dakota border. You blissfully find your way to the luggage carousel, and there they are, hunkered into their down parkas with the wool-felt lined Sorels: the Minnesotans. You run screaming back to the plane, but the door has already closed. Your fresh plumeria lei gives off its last soft fragrance as it is crushed beneath the weight of your body, sobbing on the jetway.

Pineapple Stir-Fried Rice

¼ cup oriental sesame oil
¼ cup peeled, grated fresh ginger
¼ cup finely chopped fresh lemongrass, or lemon zest
2 jalapeno chilies, finely chopped
2 tablespoons minced garlic
3 cups cooked brown rice, chilled
1½ cups peeled, finely diced pineapple
1 cup coarsely chopped fresh cilantro
⅔ cup coarsely chopped raw macadamia nuts
½ cup chopped fresh mint
2 tablespoons Thai fish sauce (nam pla)

Heat a wok or heavy large skillet over high heat. Add the first 4 ingredients and stir fry 30 seconds. Add the garlic and stir fry 30 seconds. Add the rice and cook until heated through. Add the remaining ingredients and toss until heated through. Serve.

Note: To make this dish a main course, add 12 ounces of diced shrimp or scallops at the same time as the garlic.

This recipe is from Peter Merriman of Merriman's Restaurant on the Big Island of Hawaii. It is full of complicated, exotic flavors. If you put in the seafood, or a skewer or two of grilled shrimp on top, you've got yourself a meal. If you fly over to the Big Island, hang out on the beach drinking something with an umbrella in it, and go to Peter's wonderful restaurant in Waimea for dinner; you've got yourself a vacation.

Garlic Mashed Potatoes

1 head fresh garlic
7 cups russet or Yukon Gold potatoes, peeled if you like,
   cut into 1½" chunks
1½ cups buttermilk, warm
1½ teaspoons coarse salt
salt and pepper

Cut the top ½" or so off of the garlic and put it on some aluminum foil. Sprinkle the top with olive oil and a little salt. Wrap in a little package, set it on a pie plate (so the olive oil doesn't drip in the oven) and bake it at 400° for about 30 minutes, or until the garlic is soft and paste-like. Set aside.

Put the potatoes in a pot with enough cold water to cover them by 1–2". Bring the water to a boil. Cook for 15 to 20 minutes or until the potatoes can be pierced and broken easily with a fork. Drain the potatoes and return them to the pot. Put them back on the hot burner for a few minutes to dry them. Keep stirring. Using a potato masher, mash the potatoes, adding the buttermilk a little at a time and as much garlic as you like. (The soft garlic will squeeze out of the papers like toothpaste.) I don't think the whole head would be excessive for a garlic lover. Season with salt and pepper.

Serve with one or more of these toppings:
crumbled blue cheese
onions, cooked in olive oil until caramelized
sautéed shiitake mushrooms

I love the garlic mashed potatoes that are out there, but you just know they are full of butter, don't you? This is my invention. I love buttermilk, and adding it to mashed potatoes gives them that kind of sour creamy taste we love.

National Public Radio Cranberry Sauce

2 cups raw cranberries
1 small onion
½ cup sugar
¾ cup sour cream
2 tablespoons horseradish

Grind cranberries and onion together or pulse in food processor. Stir in remaining ingredients. Freeze in covered container. The night before serving, remove from freezer and beat with a spoon. It should be thick, creamy and have some icy slivers left.

Now I'm in a Thanksgiving kind of mood. One Thanksgiving, my brother Jim called to ask how to make cranberry sauce. Unfortunately, I was out filling the bird feeder and by the time I heard his message it was late Thanksgiving evening and we were already lying around suffering from tryptophan poisoning. (That's the stuff that's in turkey that makes you tired—I'm not giving you poisonous recipes.) If I had been there to answer that call, I could have given him the recipe where you just open both ends of the can of jellied cranberry sauce and push it out, or the one on the back of the cranberry bag that has the raw cranberries and the sugar and the orange, (which is better if you add a little almond extract to it), but I think these two are good and a little more unusual.

Char Taplin's Cranberry Sauce

1 lb. cranberries
1 cup sugar
½ cup brown sugar
½ cup golden raisins
2 teaspoons cinnamon
1 teaspoon ginger
½ teaspoon nutmeg
¼ teaspoon ground cloves
¼ teaspoon allspice
1 cup water

Cook all until berries pop.

Stir in:
1 cup diced onion
1 apple, chopped
Cook until thick.

Stir in:
½ cup chopped pecans

Char gave me this recipe, but she made me promise to tell you that it came from Byerly's.

Ginger Apple Butter

2 tablespoons unsalted butter
1¼ lbs. Granny Smith apples, peeled, cored and sliced
2 cups chicken stock
⅛ cup applejack or brandy (or to taste)
¾ cup water
½ cup sugar
½ cup finely diced fresh ginger

Melt butter in skillet over high heat. Add apples and stir 3 minutes. Add stock and boil until reduced by ¾, stirring frequently, about 14 minutes. Add applejack and boil until sauce thickens, about 3 minutes. Set aside. Combine water, sugar and ginger in small saucepan and simmer until ginger is tender and liquid is reduced to a thick syrup, about 25 minutes. Puree in food processor or blender. Add to apple mixture and reheat.

Optional—sprinkle with chopped fresh chives. Swirl in some additional unsalted butter, if you don't care about your arteries.

This recipe has become an institution at Thanksgiving at our house, and I have to put it in this book. Otherwise, I might lose the 1986 *Bon Appetit* from which the original germ of the recipe came, and Dick would weep. You must double or triple this and serve it next to the turkey.

Butternut Squash Casserole

2 medium or 1 large butternut squash
2–4 tablespoons butter
salt and pepper to taste
¼ teaspoon ground ginger
2 eggs
¼ cup golden raisins (Char says don't substitute and I
   wouldn't mess with a person who feels that way about pie)
1 tablespoon crystallized ginger, finely chopped
½ cup pecan halves
2 tablespoons maple syrup

Scrub squash, cut in half lengthwise and remove seeds. Place squash, cut side down in flat pan—like a jelly roll pan. Bake at 350° until tender, about 30 minutes.

Scrape squash out of shell into food processor or mixer bowl. Add butter and seasonings; taste and adjust seasonings. Mix until smooth. Add eggs. Add raisins and crystallized ginger and mix with a spoon. Pour into buttered flat baking dish. Arrange nut halves in decorative pattern on top and drizzle maple syrup over all. Casserole can be refrigerated until 45 minutes before serving. Bake at 300° until set (at least half hour).

Every relationship has a tragic flaw, but that doesn't mean you won't have an OK time together.

Charlotte Riersgard, one of my globe-trotting Maui neighbors, gave me this recipe. It is so good, you could almost put it in a pie crust and call it dessert. That would up the fat content substantially and throw Char, who is a registered dietitian, into a frothing fit. Actually, I remember Char talking almost orgasmically about that little food zone where the pie crust meets the chocolate cream pie. I was so embarrassed I practically had to leave the room, but I do love people who are food specific.

Train Stopped in Montana

The old cars parked by the tracks in Shelby
Look like they've been there just short of forever.
Someone drove in,
Got on the train,
And never came back.
The town doesn't care.
Dusty, faded browns, sage greens,
Patches of dried alkali
Spots that had water once, who knows when.
I try to imagine living here.
There's not a sign of life except at the stockyards,
Where hundreds of horses are penned.
As the train rolls by,
I look for a good one,
But feel cold just thinking about being on a horse
In this land.

The sky is big, though, like they say.
They've got an abundance of sky.
Under it are miles of chewed down, dried out,
Rode hard, and put away wet land.
And if you were happy
Living here,
How could you possibly be
Anyplace else?

SIDE DISHES 85

Main Dishes

Grilled Chicken Breast with Cilantro Pesto and Grilled Pineapple Salsa

Pesto:
½ cup chopped cilantro
½ cup pine nuts
3 cloves garlic
5 tablespoons olive oil
salt and pepper to taste
Blend in food processor.

Salsa:
1 fresh pineapple, peeled, cored and cut into wedges 1" thick
½ cup fresh cilantro
¼ cup fresh lime juice
1 teaspoon cumin
½ teaspoon dried red chilies
3 cloves minced garlic
½ seeded, chopped red bell pepper

Grill pineapple wedges until half cooked and smoky. Finely chop the pineapple and mix with other ingredients. Let stand at room temperature while you prepare the chicken.

Cut a pocket in one chicken breast for each person you are serving. Put about 1 tablespoon pesto in breast. Close the slit with a wooden skewer or toothpick. Grill until just done. You can tell by pressing on the chicken. It should be just firm, but not dry. Remove from grill and serve topped with pineapple salsa. Rice and a black bean salad would be nice, too.

The best chicken used to come from Moris Poultry Farm near Oakdale, Minnesota. Now they have closed down, probably to make way for more tract mansions. They had breasts Dolly Parton would have if she were a chicken.

Lyle, Again

I went to see Lyle again.

At first, I didn't think I could get tickets. The concert was almost sold out and somehow, by a horrible oversight, I had not been placed on Lyle's list of friends and family.

When I called the box office they told me the only seats available were in the last row of the balcony. I didn't want to hurt Lyle's feelings by having him look up and see me crouching in a seat under the ornate rafters. It would be like seeing your old grandmother standing in the back of the church at your wedding. Not that I'm old and infirm or anything, but it would be wrong, you know?

I waited until the day before the show and called again. They told me it was still sold out, but maybe some seats would open up just before the show if some of Lyle's friends didn't come.

"*Friends*?" I asked. "What if you consider yourself a *really good* friend, even though you've never exactly met, but you know that when you *do* meet, you'll be *extremely* close.... Does that count?"

I could tell the reservation woman was listening very silently, as if she were talking with a person who might do something dangerous to themselves at any moment. Even I began to worry about my mental health.

"You'd have to talk with his agent about that," she replied, but I knew she expected to see me standing at a bus stop on Hennepin Avenue, reciting baseball statistics to total strangers sooner than I'd be talking with anybody's agent.

I quickly attempted to explain the bit about not disappointing Lyle, but she wasn't interested. That was clear.

The day of the concert, I was already dressed up and waiting on the deck when our son, John, got home from work.

"Mom, what's the deal?" he asked.

"We're going to the Lyle Lovett concert," I explained.

I'd decided to take John, because I didn't think it was fair to once again force my husband through this ordeal.

"But I thought it was sold out," John replied.

"It *is* sold out," I answered. "Hurry up and get dressed."

As we drove to Minneapolis, I refused to let the thought that we would not get seats enter my mind. I pictured us seated right in front of the stage. (Actually, I pictured myself with a T-shirt that said, in big letters, "Lyle, it's me!" and Lyle calling me up on stage, introducing me and then asking me to sing the part Emmy Lou Harris usually sings on one of his songs...but maybe I'm too visual....)

An hour before the show, I was standing in a very short line with two other people waiting for tickets. We chatted about the other concerts we had attended and which was the best location, and as much as you can strike up a friendship in four and a half minutes, we did a fair job. I actually felt kind of bad that I would have to have them killed if they got the last two tickets to the show.

Fifty-five minutes before showtime, the box office person called my line companions over and found two single tickets in the front of the balcony.

I was next.

I asked for two tickets as I turned the laminated seating chart over to the side that detailed the main floor. She tapped her computer for a minute and produced two tickets for the sixth row, dead center, in front of the stage.

We went in and sat down among people who were all wearing stickers that said "Lyle Lovett Summer Tour 2001" and "Guest." There were a couple of old people in front of us that I like to think were Lyle's grandparents. The blonde on my right must have been his cousin, Donna. The dark haired woman behind me was his sixth grade teacher.

We were with our people.

Lyle, of course, was brilliant.

Smoked Salmon Pasta

1 tablespoon olive oil
1 red onion, sliced
1 Granny Smith apple, peeled and sliced
1 cup pea pods, snow or sugar snap
¼ cup fresh chopped chives
¾ cup smoked salmon, broken into pieces
1 cup heavy cream
salt and pepper
10 oz. fettuccini, cooked

Sauté onion and apple in olive oil until lightly brown. Add pea pods and sauté until cooked but still crisp. Add chives, salmon and cream and heat through. Season to taste with salt and pepper. Toss with cooked pasta.

"It's nice to be important, but it's more important to be nice." (Mom)

I don't care if this recipe does have a cup of heavy cream in it. I could eat the whole thing myself.

Pollo Tonnato

1 carrot, peeled and sliced
1 celery stalk, sliced
½ medium onion, peeled and sliced
3 tablespoons olive oil
½ cup dry white wine
3 whole chicken breasts, split, skinned, boned and trimmed

Use a skillet just large enough to hold the chicken breasts in 1 layer. Sauté the vegetables in the oil in the skillet, covered, over low heat until veggies are wilted, about 10 minutes. Add wine and cook another 2 minutes. Add chicken, cover and cook for 10–15 minutes, depending on thickness of breasts. Let cool in the broth. Refrigerate.

Tuna Fish Sauce:
7 oz. can tuna fish
4 flat anchovy fillets
3 tablespoons capers
juice of 1 lemon
¾ cup olive oil
1 cup mayonnaise

Puree tuna, anchovies, capers, lemon juice and oil in food processor. Stir in mayonnaise to taste. Spread a platter with about half of the Tuna Fish Sauce. Arrange cold sliced chicken breasts on sauce. Cover with remaining sauce. Cover platter and refrigerate overnight. Garnish with spinach, lemon slices, capers and chopped parsley. Serves 6–8.

Lonnie Lovness gave me this recipe after one of her many trips abroad. It is a great summer main dish, but it needs a little help in the cosmetic department. (Don't we all.) You would do well to serve it on a platter garnished with fresh spinach leaves and half slices of lemon. Otherwise, unlike Lonnie, it might be frighteningly monochromatic.

Indian Chicken

1 chicken, cut into pieces and skinned
1 tablespoon tomato sauce
½ cup plain yogurt
4–5 teaspoons ground almonds
2 teaspoons lemon juice
1½ teaspoons coriander, ground
½ heaping teaspoon cumin powder
¼–½ teaspoon garam masala (Indian curry powder)
1" piece ginger root
3 cloves garlic
¼ teaspoon red chili powder—cayenne
salt to taste
2 medium onions, very finely chopped

Mix all the above ingredients except the onions (ginger root and garlic should be ground first in a food processor). Add chicken and marinate overnight in a nonmetal dish. Next day, brown the onions in ¼ cup oil, stirring frequently until onions are the color of chocolate. Add about ½ cup of water. Add chicken and marinade and cook, covered, over very low heat until tender—about 1 hour. Serve with rice.

Twice, Dick has convinced me to try living someplace with a less miserable climate than Minnesota. Both times, I made him move back. Why? Anybody can live in California. If you've got what it takes to survive here, you have a moral obligation to sign up. It was in Ukiah, California, where I took a class from an Indian woman (Gandhi, not cowboys and...) and learned to make this chicken.

Turkey Cutlets with Dried Sweet Cherry Sauce

1 boneless, skinless turkey breast
1 tablespoon olive oil
2 chopped shallots
½ cup dry red wine
¼ cup maple syrup or honey
¼ cup unsalted butter
fresh ground black pepper
½ cup dried sweet cherries, pitted

Cut turkey into ½" thick slices. Heat oil in a heavy skillet. Season turkey with salt and pepper and quickly brown in the oil. It should just be firm to the touch. Remove turkey and keep warm. Add shallots to the pan. Sauté until tender. Add red wine to the pan, scraping up bits that are stuck to the bottom. Add maple syrup or honey and any juices that have drained off the turkey and simmer until reduced to a thick cream. Swirl in butter over low heat and season with pepper. Toss in cherries and pour over turkey.

I think it's nice to have turkey sometimes when it's not Thanksgiving and you don't have to cook all day, or, if you're a kid, lie around starving and waiting for Grandma to show up so you can eat. You could serve this with mashed sweet potatoes, salad and chocolate pecan pie. You could even do it in July. What a rogue.

Cornish Hens

4 Cornish hens, halved
1½ cups soy sauce
½ cup lemon juice
1½ teaspoons ginger—I think I'd use fresh ginger today,
    probably 3 tablespoons grated
1½ cloves garlic—or more

Mix and pour over halved hens. Refrigerate overnight. Don't do this in a metal pan—a big zip-lock baggy would be nicer.

Bake in sauce at 350° for 30 minutes, covered. Uncover, turn and bake 30 minutes more.

If you're concerned about fat, don't eat the skin, or try skinning them and then baking—whatever.

This is an old recipe for Cornish game hens. I hope you don't have a sodium problem. Really, don't worry about it, it's just a marinade.

Italian Greens and Beans

1 large bunch fresh greens (spinach, Swiss chard, kale)
¼ cup olive oil
2 large onions, sliced
1 small green pepper, sliced
5 cloves garlic, minced
2 cans white, kidney, or spicy pinto beans (15 oz. each)
1 cup red pasta sauce or tomato sauce
1 cup water
½ teaspoon salt
fresh grated good parmesan cheese
balsamic vinegar (optional)

**Clean greens and coarsely chop. In a soup pan, heat olive oil
and sauté onion, green pepper and garlic until tender. Stir in
beans, pasta sauce, water and salt. Bring to a boil. Add greens
and cover. Cook just until greens are tender. Ladle into bowls.
Serve with cheese and a sprinkling of vinegar, if desired.**

Be wary of men with very small noses.

A lot of vegetarian food is awful, but what can you do about it? Most vegetarians are so nice, you can't just pelt them with tofu and storm out of the room. This hearty winter stew is delicious, spicy and beautiful. If you serve it with warm crusty bread and a good red wine, you will have made the world a better place, and saved room for cheesecake for dessert.

Poor Dead Pheasant ala Cranberry Wine Sauce

greens, like spinach or kale
6 pheasant breast halves, skinned and boned,
  (BBs picked out)
¼ cup flour
2 teaspoons coarse salt
2 teaspoons coarse ground pepper
½ cup chopped onion
⅔ cup red wine
½ cup dried cranberries
⅓ cup maple syrup
½ cup apple cider
½ teaspoon thyme
¼ teaspoon salt
½ teaspoon ground pepper

I made this one up for my brother Jim, who was sick of eating lentils. He takes his dog, Gus, out pheasant hunting and brings him back looking like he's been run over by a school bus. I think Gus deserves at least half of the pheasant. Note: Michael went nuts for this dish and he's a food snob.

Heat the oven to 375°. Chop and sauté the greens until just tender and set aside.

Smack the pheasant breasts with a rolling pin a few times to loosen them up. They may be tense. After all, they've been chased by a dog, shot and filleted. You don't want to get them paper thin or anything, just a little smacked around. Mix the flour, 2 teaspoons salt and 2 teaspoons pepper in a pie pan and dredge the breasts in it. Spray a nonstick frying pan with vegetable cooking spray. Spray a little on the dredged breasts, too.

Over medium heat, brown the pheasant breasts on both sides, until almost done; the juice will be pink if you prick the breast. Put the breasts in an ovenproof serving dish in the oven.

Spray the pan again and brown the onion. Add the wine and cranberries. Reduce to a thick syrup, but don't burn it. Add the maple syrup, cider, thyme, salt and pepper and reduce again, but not quite as much. Remove pheasant breasts from oven and add the breasts and any juice that ran off of them to the pan. Cook, turning a couple of times, to finish cooking—it should only take a few minutes. An instant read thermometer stuck in the center of a breast should read 160°, or the juice should still run, but be clear. Quickly reheat the greens, put them on the heated platter, top with pheasant and pour the sauce over it.

Artfully arranged, roadkill makes very nice table decorations.

Lobster Risotto

several cups fish or vegetable stock
2 lobster tails
2 tablespoons olive oil
⅓ cup chopped leeks
1½ cups arborio rice
1¼ cups chopped red bell pepper
½ teaspoon dried tarragon
½ cup white wine
parmesan cheese
salt and pepper

I love risotto and lobster. I invented this one night on the north shore. We served it with good bread, roasted peppers, parmesan cheese, pears and wine, of course.

Put the stock in a pan and bring to a boil. Remove the meat from the lobster tail and put the shells in the stock. Simmer for a while, covered. Chop up the lobster meat and sauté in a large frying pan with a little olive oil, until just opaque. Remove from pan and set aside. Add oil to pan and sauté leeks for a few minutes. Add rice and stir for a few more minutes. Start adding hot broth, a ladleful at a time and stir constantly until liquid is almost gone. Add more broth and stir some more. Keep this up until the rice is almost tender. Add bell pepper, tarragon and white wine. Continue stirring until rice is just done. Stir in lobster meat, grated parmesan cheese to taste, and season with salt and pepper. Serve immediately, it should be the consistency of creamy oatmeal; if it is too dry, add a little more stock.

Note: It is traditional to stir in some butter at the end, but we're watching our hips, aren't we?

Calamari with Lime and Ginger

2 large limes
2 tablespoons oriental sesame oil
2 tablespoons peanut oil
2 lbs. squid, cleaned, cut into ¼" wide pieces
salt and freshly ground pepper
2 small green onions, chopped
2 tablespoons+ finely chopped peeled fresh ginger

Remove peel and white pith from limes. Working over bowl to catch juice, cut between membranes with small sharp knife to release segments. Reserve lime segments and any juices separately in small bowls.

Heat oils in heavy skillet over medium-high heat. Season squid with salt and pepper. Add to skillet and sauté until opaque, about 1 minute. Remove from heat. Mix in onions, ginger and reserved lime juice to taste. Transfer squid to serving platter. Garnish with lime segments and serve.

This dish makes a good appetizer or a light lunch.

This recipe is from Gerard's, a fine restaurant in Lahaina, Maui, where my mind was brainwashed more than once. How do you clean squid? Cut off the tentacles, but don't include the eyes. Remove the beak if it's in there. Pull all the stuff—head, organs, etc.—out of the long sack. Pull out the backbone from the sack—it's clear cartilage. If you like, pull off the fins and the thin layer of skin over the sack. Rinse sack and tentacles. Cut sack into rings. Either sauté it quickly or braise it for a long time; in between is tough.

Leg of Lamb with Honey Lavender Sauce

3 lb. leg of lamb, deboned, trimmed and tied, save the bone
1–2 heads of garlic
olive oil
salt and pepper
fresh lavender—not sprayed with anything
honey
vegetable or chicken stock

Occasionally, it is nice to eat a helpless animal with big brown eyes and lips. I will not pass judgment. Just remember that most of the time we should be eating the helpless broccoli. I am including this recipe, because if you intend to fall off the vegetarian wagon, you might as well do it in style. And, because I learned this from Haj, the owner of the Barbary Fig Restaurant in St. Paul, Minnesota, who has beautiful big brown eyes and lips.

The day before you intend to make this dish, you have to make a good lamb stock. If you want to skip this, go to a good cooking store and buy some lamb demi-glace (condensed stock), if you can find it. Otherwise do this:

Put the lamb bone in a pan in the oven on 400°. Roast it until it is getting brown. Add some vegetables (cut up) to the pan—carrots, celery, onions—and continue roasting until the bone is really brown and the veggies are caramelized. You don't want them all black, but really dark brown. Put this in a pot and cover it with water. Throw in a few peppercorns. Simmer it for a long time. Take out the bones and veggies and continue to simmer it longer. You want to reduce it to the essence of lamb stock—demi-glace—what people used before there were yucky bouillon cubes. Save it for tomorrow.

Take a head of garlic, cut off the top ¼, put it in a small pan and drizzle it with olive oil. Roast the garlic in a 400° oven until it is soft and squishy. Take out and set aside.

Cut about three large cloves of raw peeled garlic into thin slivers. Poke little slits in the lamb and slide the garlic in. Sprinkle the outside with salt and pepper. Roast at 325–350° for 20–30 minutes a pound or 1½ hours for a 3 lb. roast. You can check it with a meat thermometer—160° for slightly rare—175° for well done. Remember that it will cook further after it is out of the oven from the residual heat, so if you want it rare, take it out a little sooner than you think and let it stand, tented with foil before you carve it. Haj checks his roast by poking it with his finger—he stops cooking it when it feels firm. This works pretty well, actually.

While the lamb is roasting, make a sauce. There are no measurements here. Sorry. Use a medium size frying pan and drizzle in a little olive oil. Squeeze in the roasted garlic a clove at a time. Stir it into the olive oil with a whisk. Put maybe a cup of stock and a half cup of the demi-glace. Boil this, whisking away, until it is reduced to a thick cream-like sauce. Stir in a couple of spoonfuls of honey and about a tablespoon of lavender flowers. Stir it around and simmer some more. Taste and change things if you like—season it with some salt and pepper. Serve the lamb, sliced, with some sauce spooned on top. A nice side dish would be couscous and/or Linda's roast veggies (pg. 72).

If a recipe fails, re-name it.

Real Southern Barbecue

Some of you have heard this story before, so suffer through it again. In about 1973, my Dad, brother Bob and I took a car trip to Florida. Aside from the fact that my dad drove like a maniac through a blizzard (he always used a good blizzard as a reason to make a major car trip) and he and Bob ate black licorice all the way there (one of the three foods I cannot handle—the others being canned okra and dates), it was a good trip. However, the highlight of trip, and probably my life, was a sandwich I had at a little open pit barbecue on the side of the road in Georgia. The place was a shack, and there is no way you can imagine just how bad it looked. Why we even went in amazes me. (On second thought, who am I kidding. If I saw a sign in the South that said "Open Pit" and a dog hadn't been licking on the food, I'd eat there.) So we went into this little falling down shack; it was just a counter, really, with a door to a back room where there was half an oil drum with smoke pouring out of it through a hole in the roof. The sandwich they brought back was tender, stringy pork with a salt and peppery taste and a hot, runny, vinegar sauce. I can still remember every bite, and no sandwich since has measured up. That is until I heard this guy on television giving the recipe for real southern barbecue, as opposed to Texas barbecue, which is the tomatoey-ketchup stuff they have most places. Not that that's bad, mind you, but it ain't southern barbecue.

Real Southern Barbecue

Buy a Boston butt roast (pork) and marinate it overnight in a mixture of cider vinegar, brown sugar, salt and black pepper. Maybe 1 cup of vinegar, ¼ cup of brown sugar, ½ teaspoon salt and 1 teaspoon pepper, for those of you who are imagination impaired.

Get the grill going. You don't need to use too many coals, just add a few every now and then to keep a low heat going. It wouldn't hurt to throw on some wet hickory chips. Grill the meat, lean side down, on top of foil for 3½ hours. Turn over and grill skin side down for an hour more. This all depends, of course, on the heat of the coals and the size of the roast. Keep those coals cool; my roast didn't take this long. You want to cook it until it will shred in strings.

Now slice and kind of chop the meat up a little so the salty outside parts get mixed in with the rest. This is not a time to worry about your health. This recipe is not about health. Season the meat with salt, pepper and a little cider vinegar. Keep it warm. You will serve it with the following sauce. Let people squeeze it on themselves. Put the sauce in a plastic ketchup or honey bottle with a big hole on the top.

The Secret Sauce:
4 cups cider vinegar
⅓ cup black pepper—yes, ⅓ cup
⅓ cup ground red pepper—ditto*
½ cup Worcestershire sauce
1 tablespoon liquid smoke
½ cup peanut oil
pinch of seasoned salt

*However, we have learned through experience, that not all red pepper is cayenne pepper. One third cup of cayenne is too much. I think they used to sell ground red pepper that was more like a chili powder. Now I use a mixture of mostly chili powder and a little cayenne, to taste. But, it should be hot.

Desserts

Hints for Healthy Living

I know people who have cholesterol higher than mine. Some of them are still alive, even, so I thought I should include a few recipes just for them. I know there are lots of books and magazines out there with recipes for healthy food, but we don't know if those recipes are any good, do we? And we don't want to stop eating our Colonel Sander's Extra Crispy long enough to find out.

This low fat, no fat thing makes me sick. There is nothing wrong with eating a little fat. It's just stupid to take your fat in the form of a Ho-Ho® or Ding-Dong®. The best fat I can think of right at this minute is the kind in the truffles at St. Paul, Minnesota's, "Just Truffles" shop. If you decide to eat something really "bad" for you, go there and get one of those. It would be best if you walked there.

A lot of people count fat grams. Not me. None of it seems relevant. Why would anyone want to know the fat grams in a half cup of Häagen Dazs? We need to know the fat grams in a *pint* of Häagen Dazs. If you can eat just a half cup of ice cream, don't worry about fat grams, you don't have a problem. Here are some facts we all should know:

Fat grams in:

1 pint of Häagen Dazs coffee ice cream: 72

1 cup of whipping cream: 96

1 cup of butter: 176

½ cup of chocolate chips, semi-sweet: 61

1 ounce of unsweetened chocolate: 14

8 ounces of cream cheese: 80

Chocolate Truffles

¼ cup whipping cream
2 tablespoons rum, brandy or any liqueur
6 ounces chopped semi-sweet chocolate
4 tablespoons unsalted butter, soft
powdered unsweetened cocoa

Boil cream in a small heavy pan until reduced to 2 tablespoons. Remove from heat, stir in rum and chocolate, and return to low heat; stir until chocolate melts. Whisk in softened butter. When smooth, refrigerate until firm, about 40 minutes. Don't forget it and let it get really hard. Scoop chocolate with a teaspoon and shape into 1" balls. Roll in unsweetened cocoa. Store, covered, in the refrigerator. Let truffles warm up 30 minutes before eating them. *Don't get cocoa powder all over the cookbook.*

In case this whole low fat idea is not for you, and you're already breaking out in a sweat just thinking about it, make these and eat them while you read the book. Go ahead. It's part of your therapy.

Carroll's Prunes

3 dozen prunes or more
1 bottle (4 cups) port wine*
¾ cup sugar
1 vanilla bean
whipped cream
amaretti cookies

Put prunes in a nonmetal bowl and cover with 2 cups of the wine. Refrigerate 24 hours. Combine with the remaining wine, sugar and vanilla bean and simmer until the prunes are plump, about 1 hour. Cool and store, covered, in the refrigerator for 3 days or more. Serve in wine glasses with whipped cream and an amaretti cookie on the side. As Carroll so correctly observed, "the liquid is the best part."

*This is one of those times that you don't want to buy a real cheap port, but you wouldn't need to buy a really good port to cook prunes in either, would you? You should just plain old drink a real good port. Also, amaretti cookies are plentiful at Italian markets such as Buon Giorno Italian Market in St. Paul, Minnesota. If you don't live in Minnesota, I don't know where you will get your amaretti.

You'll need to be sitting down to read this. This is a low fat recipe. It is still good, though, and if you serve it with whipped cream, you'll be OK. It came from Carroll Davis-Johnson, who is a good writer and cook. I think this is best served in the winter when the need to drown one's remorse in good food and alcohol is strongest.

Jim's Berry Pie

9–11 sheets of phyllo dough (available in the frozen bread
    section of your grocery store)
vegetable oil spray (I like to use the new Spectrum spray
    canola oil)
sugar
5 cups fresh blackberries, although I'm sure you could use
    blueberries, raspberries, etc.
½–1 cup sugar, to taste
1 tablespoon lemon juice
2 tablespoons water
1½ tablespoons cornstarch

Thaw and handle phyllo dough according to package directions.

Preheat the oven to 350°.

**Put berries, sugar, lemon juice, water and cornstarch in a heavy
large saucepan. Gently heat and stir until liquid boils and thickens and berries are cooked, but not mush. Taste it part way and
see if you want more sugar. (Berries vary, right?) Remove from
heat and let cool.**

**Spray a pie plate with vegetable oil spray. Lay one sheet of
phyllo on the pie plate. Spray with oil. Sprinkle with sugar. Fold
over extra pastry so it makes a square sort of circumscribed
about the circle. (A little geometry talk there. It comes in handy
sometimes. This is the first time for me since high school.)
Repeat this procedure, with pastry, oil, sugar and folding—**

I developed this recipe for my brother
after he had heart surgery. I think it's
pretty darn good. Serve it warm.

each time laying the sheet at a slight, jaunty angle to the last one, so they don't all line up. After about 7–9 layers—you may bore easily—stop and put in the berry filling. Take the extra couple of sheets of phyllo and do the same oil & sugar deal on the counter, fold the sheets in half and cut them into strips with a scissors. Decorate the top of the pie with the layered strips. Roughly fold in the edges of the pie crust to cover the ends of the strips and make a wild kind of edge. We can't do Martha Stewart here. It should look more like Barney did it.

Bake for 20-30 minutes, until deep golden brown. Serve warm or the crust will get mushy; however, we had good luck reheating it to crisp up the crust.

If you bake well, there are a lot of other things you
should not be expected to do at all.

Apples with Gjetost Cheese

3 crisp, tart, juicy baking apples, cored, peeled and halved
   lengthwise
¾ cup coarsely grated gjetost cheese
1 tablespoon coarse, raw sugar
¼ teaspoon ground cinnamon

**Heat oven to 350°. Slice apples ¼". Put slices into an oil
sprayed shallow baking dish, fanning each one. Sprinkle with
cheese. Mix sugar and cinnamon and sprinkle over all. Bake
about 25 minutes until apples are tender and cheese is melted.
Serve warm.**

I am eternally grateful that my kids
gave up soccer for video games and beer
before they invented the term "soccer mom."

You either like gjetost or you don't.
It's a caramel colored, dense, smooth
cheese from Norway. It's undoubtedly
full of fat, but this recipe uses so little cheese that overall it's a healthy
dessert.

Baked Pears with Blue Cheese and Port

2 Bosc or Bartlett pears, peeled, halved and cored
¼ cup port
¼ cup honey
2 tablespoons good blue cheese

Preheat oven to 375°. Cut a slice off the convex side of each pear half so it will lay flat in the pan. Arrange cored side up in 8" square baking dish. Combine port and honey and stir until blended. Spoon over pears. Bake until pears are tender, basting occasionally, 50 minutes.

Place rounded 1½ teaspoons cheese in center of each pear. Return to oven until cheese begins to soften, about 1 minute. Transfer pears to plates. Spoon pan juices over pears, 2 servings; can be doubled or tripled.

This is another dessert recipe that has a little bit of cheese in it. Don't worry about it. You used to eat a whole bag of cheese-its, didn't you? Eat the pears. If you just hate blue cheese, bake the pears and serve them with some vanilla yogurt in the center.

My Mom's Hot Fudge Sauce

1 cup sugar (white or half white/half brown)
⅓ cup evaporated milk
¼ cup butter
2 oz. unsweetened baking chocolate, chopped up
pinch salt

Combine everything in a saucepan and stir over medium heat until it boils. Boil one minute. Serve over ice cream.

Elaine Gonzales, Supreme Goddess of the Chocolate Religion, has a wonderful book about chocolate. She has many suggestions, but two stand out: 1. Never heat dark chocolate above 120°, nor milk and white chocolate above 110°. Chocolate will melt between 86° and 90°, don't abuse it with too much heat. 2. Never use chocolate chips unless you're making cookies. Use chocolate from the candy aisle and chop it up. There. Now I just hope I can correct all the chocolate mistakes I have made in the past.

Caramel Sauce

1 cup butter
1¾ cups sugar
2 cups whipping cream

Melt butter over-medium high heat and add sugar. Stir mixture until it has reached a deep caramel color. Remove from heat and slowly add cream. Use an oven mitt and a long-handled spoon to avoid the steam that will be produced. Stir or whisk until smooth. Strain sauce into container and refrigerate. Warm to serve.

Don't wear shoes that hurt your feet.

Oh, no. I feel kind of guilty.
A friend gave me this recipe about fourteen years ago. It was just the sauce part to a more complicated dessert and he made me swear never to give the recipe away, but I don't think I swore not to give any part of it away. Go ahead and torture me with red ants, I will never tell you the recipe for the other part.
I hope that counts.

Chocolate Chestnut Pate

¾ cup butter—unsalted
½ cup sugar
2 cups canned chestnut puree
12 oz. semi-sweet chocolate, melted*
2 tablespoons brandy
¼ teaspoon vanilla

Cream butter and sugar well, mix in the rest of the ingredients. Spread in a 9x5" loaf pan that has been lined with plastic wrap or foil so you can lift the pate out later. Chill until firmly set. Cut in ½" slices and serve as previously instructed.

*A few thoughts about melting chocolate. Melt chocolate in a microwave, on low heat, for 30 seconds at a time, stirring when you check it until it is shiny and partly melted. Take out and stir until it is smooth. Don't ever stir chocolate with a wooden spoon that could be slightly damp. It will make the chocolate seize up (get lumpy). Or, put chocolate in a warm oven in a Pyrex cup to melt. Stir when the pieces are shiny. White chocolate is more likely to seize up than dark chocolate, so be more careful. If you use squares of chocolate, always chop it up before you try to melt it. Those "chocolate coatings" wouldn't seize up if you heated them with a blow torch, but that doesn't mean we want to eat that stuff, does it?

You get what you pay for, so sometimes it's nice if you don't know the difference.

This is a delicious recipe that is wonderful as an elegant dessert after a really good dinner where you need something chocolate. However, in order to make it, you have to get chestnut puree, which is a little pricey and available at specialty food stores. (Or, you could take a trip to Italy and they would have it there.) If you want to blow them out of the water with presentation, put some chocolate and/or caramel sauce (I just gave you a recipe for caramel sauce) in one of those old honey squeeze bottles you've been saving for God knows what reason. Squirt it around on the plate in an artful abstract fashion, top it with a slice of pate and perhaps a bit of whipped cream. A little piece of mint or violet stuck into the cream would look nice, too, but you know that.

Strawberries with Marscapone Cheese

the best, most flavorful strawberries
raw sugar
1 pt. marscapone cheese*
¼–½ cup grated semi-sweet chocolate

Clean strawberries, halve and sprinkle with some raw sugar. Mix cheese with a heaping tablespoon of additional sugar and the grated chocolate. Put berries in a wine glass. Top with cheese mixture.

*Marscapone cheese availability seems to be inversely proportionate to the Cool Whip consumption in any particular area of the U.S.A. Check the government statistics for your region before attempting to procure marscapone.

All roads lead to Lucca, but only one
road leads back. (John Gordon)

On our trip to Italy, we became so miserably lost that when we finally found our house we were so grateful to be there and we never wanted to venture out again. However, hunger and curiosity prevailed and we took baby steps out into the insane world of the Italians. I quickly became very fond of the market in Barga where I could buy little bouquets of baby artichokes and incredibly wonderful strawberries. The cheeses and procuitto were excellent, too, and reaffirmed a philosophy of cooking that many hold today: Buy the best ingredients first and then decide what you can make with them. We enjoyed this invented dessert many times at the villa looking over "our" valley in Tuscany.

The Climber's Mother

Like a fly on a windowscreen,
the climber sticks
to the sheer rock face of the canyon.
High up,
very high up,
so high up,
to see him I have to lean on my car
to keep from falling over backwards.
He moves so slowly it is imperceptible.
He is there all day,
all night,
sleeping like a bat hung upside down,
held by large metal hooks in the rock,
all the blood rushing to his head,
causing damage to the judgment
center of the brain.
Where is his mother?
Now that common sense has failed him?
Making meatloaf? With a glaze of ketchup
and little bits of onion?

Making a pie?
Mixing flour, salt and lard
with two butter knives
cutting and turning
until it is time to add iced water
with her hands now
quickly so the pastry will be tender.
She reaches for the rolling pin
where the color has almost
worn away
from the painted handles.

French Silk Pie

½ cup butter
¾ cup sugar
2 squares unsweetened chocolate, melted
2 eggs or pasteurized raw egg equivalents
½ pint whipping cream, whipped with 2 tablespoons sugar
baked 8" pie crust

Beat butter, sugar and chocolate till fluffy. Add one egg and beat for 3 minutes. Add other egg and beat 3 minutes more. Fold in whipped cream. Pour into pie crust. Refrigerate until firm, or freeze to save.

French Silk Pie is made with raw eggs. I have always enjoyed living dangerously in this way, but I recently heard a nutritionist on the radio talking about the New Salmonella and how we should not eat raw eggs anymore. I tested it out and this recipe works fine with those pasteurized eggs that come in cartons, in case you are squeamish about killing your friends.

Chocolate Pecan Chess Pie

1¼ cups sugar
¼ cup cocoa powder, unsweetened
¼ cup butter, melted, unsalted would be best
2 eggs
10 tablespoons evaporated milk
1½ teaspoons vanilla or rum
⅛ teaspoon salt
1½ cups pecan pieces

Preheat the oven to 350°. Mix the above ingredients and pour into an unbaked 8" pie shell. Bake, on the bottom rack of the oven, on a cookie sheet for 35–45 minutes or until a knife comes out clean.

Nobody is as happy or as miserable as they let on.

One time I went out canoeing in the BWCA with Dick and some other people, I am sure. I can't remember who they were right now because at the time I was obsessed with a terrible mistake I had made. I thought that it would be a good idea to only eat healthy food on the trip. So, I didn't bring any chocolate. Of course, all I could think of for those four miserable days in the pristine wilderness was chocolate. When we finally paddled back to shore it was raining and windy and we were freezing, but we had lunch in a little restaurant in Ely, Minnesota, and they served a pie like this. *Warm.* Need I say more, except to quote Dorothy Deetz, who said of another dessert, "This is so good I could roll in it."

Buttermilk Raisin Pie

¼ cup cornstarch
⅔ cup sugar
¼ teaspoon salt
2 cups buttermilk
¼ cup raisins
2 tablespoons lemon juice
2 egg yolks
1 tablespoon butter
baked 8" pie shell

Mix cornstarch, sugar and salt in top of double boiler; add buttermilk, raisins and lemon juice and cook over direct heat, stirring constantly until mixture boils and thickens. Beat egg yolks until thick, stir in a little of the hot mixture, then pour back into top of double boiler. Place over boiling water and cook 2 minutes longer, continuing to stir. Remove from heat and stir in butter until melted. Cool slightly, then pour into cooled baked pie shell. Cool thoroughly before cutting. Serve with whipped cream.

Sour cream raisin pie must be a Minnesota thing, but when I want a piece, nothing else will do. This recipe uses buttermilk, but it is very much the same, and we like it. I found this in an ancient cookbook, called, ironically, *The Modern Family Cookbook*. If you ever need a bunch of recipes for meat sundries, it's your book.

Fruit Cream Tart

1½ cups unbleached flour
¼ cup powdered sugar
¾ cup butter
12 oz. cream cheese, cold
1 cup powdered sugar
1 cup heavy cream
2 tablespoons vanilla

Cut butter into flour and sugar. Mix with fingers just until it holds together. Press into a 10" springform or tart pan. Bake at 350° for about 20 minutes until just golden. Cool.

Beat cream cheese and sugar until fluffy. Slowly beat in cream and vanilla until fluffy. Remove crust from outer ring of pan. You can leave the bottom under it. Place on serving platter.

Mound in the cream filling. Top with fresh fruit—strawberries, raspberries, kiwi, whatever is nice, but doesn't weep too much. Cover with a glaze made from 1 cup jelly of an appropriate color and 4 tablespoons water, warmed in a saucepan. Refrigerate.

This recipe is a good thing to know. You can head off in lots of different directions and they will all be delicious.

Balk Sister's Poppy Seed Cake

¾ cup milk (scalding)
¾ cup poppy seeds
1½ cups sugar
¾ cup butter
2 cups flour
1½ teaspoons baking powder
4 egg whites

Preheat oven to 350°. Grease and flour 9x13" pan or 2 round layer pans. Pour scalding milk over poppy seeds and let set until cool. Cream sugar and butter. Add cooled milk and seed mixture. Blend in flour that has been mixed with baking powder. Beat egg whites until stiff and gently fold into the batter. Bake 30–40 minutes for 9x13" or 25–30 for layer pans. It's done when a toothpick pushed into the center comes out clean.

I have been known to make a fancy dessert or two. This is not a fancy one, but it is excellent because it tastes so unlike a cake mix cake. The frosting, which must be refrigerated, (even when it's on the cake, Marilyn), is one of the true comforts in this cruel world. This recipe was shared with me by Marilyn Franzini. It is from her mother's side of the family, the Balk sisters.

Frosting:
1½ cups milk
¾ cup sugar
4 egg yolks
1 teaspoon vanilla
2 tablespoons cornstarch

Stir above in sauce pan and cook very gently until thick.
Add:
1 cup coconut

Cool slightly and spread on cooled cake. Sprinkle additional coconut on top.

Note: Marilyn, in her infinite wisdom, always doubles the recipe for the frosting so she can put a lot on top. No one ever complains.

Killing the Dog

I stumble on pets. Unlike people who decide it's time to get a new puppy or kitten, carefully research and study breeds, and shop around for the perfect pet, mine just come into my life.

Maybe a dog isn't getting along with the other dogs in the family, the owners want to give him away, and I just happen to be dogless. Or my friend's 23-year-old cat dies and I bring her a new one that I picked up at the pound, but she doesn't want another cat, and it becomes mine. Or I am working for a veterinarian, and they are going to put a dog to sleep because it is a stray that no one wants, but the dog looks at me with eyes that say "I have lived on this planet before, and it was not as a dog," and I take it home in my '69 VW Beetle.

It is always like this. A little different story each time, but the end is always the same. They come to me and they stay to record age. The last was Rose. She was the result of a marital argument that sent me stomping off with the two kids. Out of spite, I took Dick's new car. It was a Sunday, and we went out to breakfast, then drove to a nearby animal shelter. (This sounds as if there is some formula to having a fight on a Sunday morning, as if Saturday morning would require a trip to the hardware store and an ice cream. There is no reason. No plan. This is just a setup for a random act of animal procurement, but I am ahead of myself.)

There we were at the shelter, walking up and down the kennel aisles of barking dogs. Not shopping. Just looking, but somehow Rose caught my eye. I must have passed by her three times before she got tired of running in and out of the little doggie door that divided the inside run from the outside. When I was inside, she was out. When I was out, she was in. Finally there she was, quivering in the corner of the run, tired of the terrifying game, willing to wait it out in one place, no doubt expecting the worst. What could I do?

She was a black and white beagle/terrier mix. She had no name; we called her Rose after Rose Kennedy because something about her looked like a Boston Terrier. She cost $65.00. Halfway home, she threw up on the backseat of my husband's new car. Oops. After a cleanup stop, we arrived home to make up.

"It's a joke, right?" was all Dick said as we walked in the door with the new dog. He got to like her, though, and she liked him too, but she adored me. Rose protected me from threats that only she could perceive: holding onto a plumber's pant leg if she thought he was too close, or leaping after my brother's rear end when his play looked like a move on me and the boys. We could never scold her for her attempts to set the world right. She was so shy in general, these raids on my aggressors must have taken years off of her life. Now that I think about it, maybe the sporadic acts of aggression made her live longer. Rose went on and on and on.

Like an old car, parts of her rusted out. Her eyes went first. Sometimes she even barked at me until she heard my voice. The vision deal seemed somewhat inconsistent, because she never fully lost the ability to see flying pieces of food. When Rosie's hearing went, I used to stomp on the kitchen floor to call her. She would feel the vibrations and come running. When her eyes started looking a little asymmetrical and her breath smelled really bad, I figured she was on her last legs, but those legs were evidently in great shape. Every morning, I'd get up and Rose would spin around waving her front paws in the air in anticipation of a cup of dog food.

Deafness and blindness convinced her that it was occasionally OK to relieve herself on the Oriental rug in the living room, even when we were sitting right next to it. Evidently she couldn't see or hear us, but you can't consider putting a dog to sleep who still dances like she is in the circus. I took her and had her teeth cleaned instead. For a sixteen-year-old dog, she had beautiful teeth.

When a small problem with nighttime nosebleeds and sniffling started, the vet said she probably had some kind of tumor behind her eye, but there was nothing we could do about it. The dancing dog persisted. We rolled up the Oriental rug, had it cleaned and stored.

"Rosie," I said, as we rested our feet on the cold wood floor, "You've had a good life. Anytime you want to leave us, would be OK. I mean, we love you Rose, but don't make yourself suffer on our account." She took a little whiz in her sleep and rolled over so I could wipe it up.

Do you really want me to tell you how it ends? That she urped in the middle of a fancy dinner party and that was it? That the next day we put her body in a Rubbermaid blanket container and buried her with the rest of the team? Of course, we all cried. For weeks after, we stumbled over the shadow of an old black dog that wasn't even there.

Coconut Pecan Filling for German Chocolate Cake

1 egg, beaten
5 oz. (⅔ cup) evaporated milk
⅔ cup sugar
¼ cup butter
1⅓ cups coconut
½ cup pecans, chopped

Cook egg, milk, sugar and butter over medium heat until thick and bubbly, about 12 minutes. Stir in coconut and pecans. Cool. Spread liberally between layers and on top of cake.

John wanted German Chocolate Cake for his birthday one year and I could find a recipe for the cake, but I'll be damned if I could find a recipe for that frosting. I started thinking we live in a little isolated pocket of German Chocolate Cake eaters and the rest of the world is oblivious to our pleasure. Just as well. After searching my cookbooks for a recipe, my friend Lisa came up with one. Bless her. (I had to bless her, because I swore earlier in this paragraph.)

German Chocolate Cake

4 oz. Baker's German Sweet Chocolate
½ cup boiling water
1 cup butter
2 cups sugar
4 eggs, separated
1 teaspoon vanilla
2¼ cups sifted flour
1 teaspoon baking soda
½ teaspoon salt
1 cup buttermilk

Stir chocolate into very hot water until it melts. Cool. Cream butter and sugar until fluffy. Add egg yolks, one at a time, beating well after each. Blend in vanilla and chocolate. Sift flour with soda and salt; add alternately with buttermilk to chocolate mixture, beating after each addition until smooth. Beat egg whites until stiff; fold in beaten whites. Pour into three 9" layer pans, lined on bottoms with parchment paper. Bake 350° for 30–35 minutes. Cool. Frost between layers and on top.

How cheeky of me to assume you just happen to have a recipe for German Chocolate Cake laying around. Sorry. Here's one to hold up the frosting. It's from the Baker's Chocolate box.

Crazy Cake

2¼ cups flour
1½ cups sugar
¼ cup cocoa
1 teaspoon salt
1½ teaspoons soda
1½ tablespoons vinegar
1 teaspoon vanilla
½ cup oil
1½ cups water

Put flour, sugar, cocoa, salt and soda in a dry 9x13" cake pan. Stir to mix. Make 3 holes in the flour mixture. Isn't this fun? Put the vinegar in one hole, the vanilla in another and the oil in the third. Pour water over the whole thing and blend. Don't worry if it has a few lumps. Bake at 350° for 25–30 minutes.

Filling:
½ cup milk
2½ tablespoons flour
½ cup butter
½ cup sugar
¼ teaspoon salt
½ teaspoon vanilla

Cook milk and flour to a thick paste. Cool. Cream butter, sugar and salt; add milk mixture a tablespoon at a time and beat until fluffy. Add vanilla. Let set for ½ hour. Spread on cake.

Frosting:
2 tablespoons butter
2 squares unsweetened chocolate, melted
3 tablespoons hot milk
1½ cups powdered sugar
1 teaspoon vanilla
dash salt

Beat together. Spread on filling.

Yes, I am still queen of the fancy dessert. But I could not exist without an occasional piece of Crazy Cake.

The original recipe has a filling and a frosting. If you baked it in the 9x13" pan, you put the filling on top of the cake and the frosting on top of the filling.

You could also mix this in a bowl and pour the batter in two 9" layer pans and bake for 18–22 minutes, if you want a birthday cake. Then I'd do two thin layers of filling and frosting on each layer.

Sara's Apple Pudding Cake

¼ cup butter or vegetable oil
1 cup sugar
1 egg
1 cup flour
½ teaspoon salt
1 teaspoon cinnamon
1 teaspoon baking soda
4 cups chopped apples* (the original recipe called for
  3–4 apples, I use way more)
½ cup raisins or dried cranberries
½ cup chopped nuts or a little more

Sara Johnson, a very good cook, brought this cake to the mom's retreat. It has no chocolate in it and I have made it several times. That says something right there. I've made a few adaptations so far, just because I can't leave anything alone.

Cream butter, sugar and egg. Stir in rest of ingredients. Bake in a 9x9" pan that has been sprayed with oil, at 350° for 1 hour. Serve with the topping of your choice, or this sauce: ¼ butter, ½ cup cream or evaporated milk, ½ cup brown sugar, ½ cup sugar; boil 1 minute, stir in 1 teaspoon vanilla.

*It has been discovered that this makes a great rhubarb cake by simply substituting chopped rhubarb for the apples. (I use raisins with rhubarb.)

Indian Persimmon Pudding

1 cup mashed persimmon pulp, coarse fibers removed
1 cup sugar
2 eggs
¼ cup butter, melted, or vegetable oil
½ teaspoon vanilla
3 tablespoons evaporated milk
¾ cup low fat buttermilk
¾ cup flour
½ teaspoon each baking powder and baking soda
¼ teaspoon cinnamon
⅛ teaspoon salt

Combine first 5 ingredients. Beat in milk and buttermilk. Add dry ingredients. Beat until nearly smooth. Pour into an 8" square pan that has been sprayed with nonstick cooking spray. Bake at 325° for 50 minutes or just until set. Serve warm or at room temperature with whipped cream or whatever.

If you find yourself worrying about what people will think, you should find some new people.

One time I had Indian Pudding at the top of the Walker Art Center in their little restaurant. It was memorable.... This pudding reminds me of that. If you like things simple and comforting, you will like it, too.

Lime Tart

Crust:
1 cup flour
½ cup unsalted butter
2 tablespoons sugar
pinch salt

Place all ingredients in a food processor. Process until the mixture just forms a ball and pat into greased 9" tart pan (or 8" square pan for bars). Bake at 375° for 15–20 minutes.

Filling:
1 cup sugar, stirred together with 1 tablespoon plus
   1 teaspoon cornstarch
½ cup fresh squeezed lime juice
2 large eggs
1 tablespoon grated lime rind
½ teaspoon baking powder

Process all ingredients in food processor. Pour into crust and bake for 20 minutes more at 375°. Cool, then chill well. Serve, cut in wedges. Top with whipped cream and fresh raspberries.

Confession: I turned that old recipe for lemon squares into a fancy dessert tart with a few changes. I served it with whipped cream and raspberries and everybody got goofy over it. Go ahead and bake these as bars if you like, but don't forget the tart when you need a quick dessert.

Yummy Dessert

6 egg whites
1¾ cups sugar
1 pint whipping cream
1 tablespoon sugar
12 Heath Bars, crushed

Beat egg whites until stiff. Slowly add 1¾ cups sugar and continue to beat to stiff peaks. Line two 9x13" pans with parchment paper, or if you want to be fancy and change the name of my dessert to something like Cotswald Cream Tart, draw a couple of 12" circles on parchment paper and put them on a baking sheet. Dividing the meringue in two equal parts, gently swirl it on the parchment, in a rectangular or circular fashion. Bake 40–45 minutes at 325°. Cool. Gently remove parchment paper. Whip cream, sweetening with 1 tablespoon sugar as you beat. Fold in crushed Heath Bars. Spread cream between layers of meringue. Cover with plastic wrap and refrigerate overnight.

My mom used to make this dessert back in the 60s. I wish I could say that I've become so sophisticated that I don't like it anymore, but that's not true. I think it's kind of like the famous Pavlova dessert named for the ballet dancer. (I'm trying to justify eating something that is mostly whipped cream and crushed Heath Bars....) The title is so embarrassing.

Cookies and Candies

Candied Orange Peel

3 ORGANIC oranges—you don't want to eat all that junk they
   spray on the oranges, do you?
1 cup sugar
2 teaspoons light corn syrup
½ cup water
more sugar

**Quarter oranges and remove peel. Save orange flesh for another
use. (Make a nice smoothie with the orange, vanilla non-fat
yogurt and a little honey.) Put the peel in a pan and cover it
with water. Boil for ½ hour. Drain. Cover again with water. Boil
½ hour longer or until tender. Drain. Cut peel into strips. Bring 1
cup sugar, corn syrup and ½ cup water to a boil. Add the peel
and cook gently in syrup until peel is clear. Cool in syrup several hours or overnight. Reheat. Drain. Roll in granulated sugar.
Dry on waxed paper. Store in a covered container. You can also
do this recipe with grapefruit or lemon peel. You could dip one
end of the candied orange peels in melted dark chocolate. I
don't think I'd like chocolate with grapefruit.**

This one is from my Grandma Olson.
Her name conjures up images that I
must assure you are false. She was a
bit of a wild woman. (*My* grandmother?) I don't want to go into all
the details right here, but trust me,
this candy was one of the only truly
grandmotherly things she did.

Jamaican Toasted Coconut Cookies

1 cup butter
1 cup sugar
½ teaspoon vanilla
1 cup coconut
½ teaspoon baking soda
1½ cups flour

Cream butter and sugar, add vanilla, coconut, baking soda and flour. Roll into 1" balls.

Press very thin with a flour-dipped fork. Bake at 250° on a lightly greased baking sheet for 30 minutes or until coconut is toasted.

When I was in sixth grade, my mother made a dropped waist, pleated dress of turquoise and cream checked fabric that I loved so much I continued to wear it the fall of seventh grade. My legs, that year, grew a great deal, while the dress remained exactly the same size. I tried to camouflage this fact by wearing cream colored opaque tights, but the dress, even for 1966, was too short. One of my teachers called me to her desk to point this out to me in a hissing whisper that branded itself on my brain. To her credit, this same teacher taught us how to make these cookies, partially redeeming herself in my mind. Always, however, be careful what you say to junior high students. They do not forget.

Macaroons

We discovered these macaroons at the farmer's market in Kona on the Big Island of Hawaii. They are perfect, at or instead, of any meal. Many times I have had one or two for breakfast.

We learned they came from a particular bakery outside of Kona. Once, when friends were visiting the Big Island, we asked them to pick up some macaroons and bring them back to Minnesota. They started sampling in the airport and polished them off on the plane. So Dick brought some to me after one of his multitude of trips to the Islands.

I slowly studied them one at a time. I noticed how white and crunchy they are on the outside. How the coconut is golden brown on the outside and soft and chewy on the inside. How they are not too sweet with not a trace of sweetened condensed milk. I went to the net and researched every coconut macaroon recipe known to man. Nothing even close. I decided on the devious route. I dialed the telephone number of the bakery in question.

"Aloha, bakery," the cheerful voice on the other side of the world answered.

"Hello," I started tentatively. "My husband bought me some of your macaroons...but I'm allergic to wheat flour.... Could you tell me if there's any flour in them?" I was grateful, once again, that I am not Catholic.

"Kalika!" she yelled to the back of the bakery, "is there flour in the macaroons?"

I heard the answer before she even had time to repeat it to me, "No, there's just egg whites, sugar, cornstarch and coconut."

Forgive me father, for I have sinned.

Bless you, Kalika.

This recipe is pretty darn close.

Kona Macaroons

¾ cup warm water
¼ cup Just Whites* (dried egg whites)
pinch cream of tartar
1⅓ cups sugar
½ teaspoon vanilla
½ cup cornstarch
14 oz. fancy shredded coconut
parchment paper**

You can never thank me enough for this recipe, but I suppose you could try. Chocolates would be a nice start.

*I developed this recipe with the dried egg whites. However, you can use fresh whites instead. Use 6 large egg whites instead of the water and dried whites.

**You can get parchment paper at the grocery store in the baking section or by the waxed paper.

Put water and dried egg whites in a mixer bowl with a whisk attachment if you have it. If you don't, not to worry, it will be fine. Add cream of tartar and beat until it forms soft peaks. Scrape the bowl. Add sugar a little at a time as you continue beating to stiff peaks. This means that if you lift up the beater, the egg white mixture will make little pointy mountains whose tops do not droop over. Beat in the vanilla. Toss the coconut with the cornstarch and fold gently into the egg whites.

Cover two big cookie sheets with parchment paper, spray it with vegetable oil spray and dust with cornstarch. Use a spring type ice cream scoop, if you have one, to dole out roughly round shapes of coconut mix that are about ¼ cup each. You should get about 24 mounds. Whatever, don't sweat it. Bake them at 300° for about 1 hour. When they are done, the tops are slightly cracked, the coconut is golden, the crust is firm, but still very light. Take the pans out of the oven and cool. Remove from parchment paper when cool and firm.

Kathy's Biscotti

1 cup oil
1½ cups sugar
4 eggs, beaten
1½ teaspoons almond extract
1 tablespoon lemon juice
½ teaspoon baking soda
4 cups flour
1 cup sliced almonds

Our Italian-Jewish friend, Kathy Koch, may be a genetically perfect cook. This recipe is actually from her best friend's daughter's mother-in-law, but really, let's just call it Kathy's.

Mix oil and sugar, beat well. Add beaten eggs, beat again. Add almond extract. Mix lemon juice with soda, add to mixture. Add flour slowly. Dough will be soft. Add almonds. Divide dough into 3 or 4 parts. On a floured surface, shape dough into rolls ½" thick, 2" wide and as long as your cookie sheet. Place no more than two rolls on each ungreased cookie sheet. Bake 20 minutes at 375°. Remove from oven and remove carefully from sheet. Cut into ½" slices, place side by side, back on baking sheet. Bake 10–15 minutes. Turn and bake for another 10–15 minutes or until golden brown. You can make many variations of these: chocolate chip, raisin, cranberry, etc. You can also dip half of the cookie in melted chocolate.

I was born at night, but it wasn't last night.

Miscellaneous

Dog Biscuits

3½ cups whole wheat flour
2 cups white flour
1 cup oatmeal
2 cups corn meal
2 teaspoons salt
2 bunches of fresh parsley, altogether, the size of a soccer ball
1 small bunch of fresh mint, grapefruit sized
2 cups hot water
2 bouillon cubes
2 large eggs, whisked

Preheat oven to 325.

In a large bowl, mix together flours, oat and corn meal, and salt. Mince the herbs very fine. The only way I would have patience to do this is in the food processor, but if mincing parsley by hand is your thing, have at it. Dissolve the bouillon cubes in the water, stir in the herbs and eggs. Slowly stir in the flour mixture, kneading with your hands when you can't stir any longer. Or, use the dough hook attachment on your handy Kitchen Aid mixer. Roll out to a thickness of ¼–½" on a lightly floured board. Use doggie shape cookie cutters and place on lightly greased cookie sheet—they don't spread. Bake for 45 minutes. Then turn off the oven and leave the biscuits in the oven overnight or for 8 hours. Store the biscuits airtight. Makes many dozen, depending on the size of your cookie cutters.

Dogs should be seen and not smelled.

It seems that every Christmas season, friends show up at my door with unexpected gifts like certificates for a vacation in Europe or mid-sized sport utility vehicles. I always feel so foolish if I don't have something to give in return.

Then it came to me. While many of them had thoughtfully remembered their pet with a sable waistcoat and perhaps eel skin booties, the holiday pastry tray was lacking when it came to the canine companions.

A well-mannered dog would never think of sneaking a rosette, truffle or rum-soaked sugar plum, even if nobody is looking. However, he will take note, and, at Easter, if your basket contains only wrappers, drool, and a few of those marshmallow peeps that Martha persuaded you to make, don't say I didn't warn you.

Fumble

He bounced for thirteen years
Though the white muzzle
Gave him away.
He didn't own a mirror
Didn't know how an old dog
Should act,
Until I found him in the garage
Where he couldn't get up.
We carried him
Into the house.

I tempted him,
A dry food kind of dog,
With bits of meat
From a can.
For this he went on two more months,
And one last walk.
But still he failed.

We called the vet,
And dug a hole
In the orchard,
Through an early snowfall,
And laid him there
Glazed with tears
Left gifts of toys and tennis balls
For the journey.
Because we didn't know
If he was a Christian dog
Or some other religion,
He had tremendous faith
But it was just
In us.

Homemade Playdough

½ cup salt
1 cup water
1 cup flour
2 teaspoons cream of tartar
1 tablespoon oil
food coloring

Mix everything except food coloring in a medium saucepan and stir over low heat until it makes a dough. Remove from heat and stir in coloring. Knead. Cool. Store in a covered container.

Modeling your child rearing method after that of the Snow Monkey is probably as good as any.

When you have little kids, people always tell you how fast they grow up. You are so busy washing diapers and wiping poop off of butts, it's hard to appreciate this fact. However, it is true. One minute they are five, and 5,256,000 minutes later, are getting their driver's permit and don't want you around anymore. Playdough making is a small price to pay for complete adoration.

Separation Anxiety

When you were new,
your body was ripe apricots
with little prune feet.
I knew the print
of your downy head on my palm
like no other,
I could swallow you with my heart,
protect you with my being.
Know this
as you strain away from home
and I practice learning
to let you go.

INDEX

About the Author

Lori Powell Gordon was born in 1954 in Stillwater, Minnesota, to a nice Methodist couple.

Unable to master the slide rule, she studied art at the Universities of Minnesota and Wisconsin. After brief careers in kennel maintenance, envelope stuffing, and motherhood, she worked several years as a photo stylist for some of the biggest boxed dinner purveyors on Earth.

Retired from the advertising world, Ms. Gordon enjoys writing and dreams of becoming a baitshop owner/operator and country western star.

She lives in Scandia, Minnesota with her extremely tolerant husband and two sons.

She weighed ten pounds, eleven and three-quarters ounces at birth.

144